# JOHN

## ALEXA TEWKESBURY

## CWR

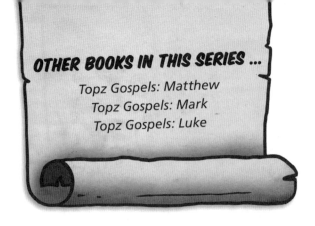

OTHER BOOKS IN THIS SERIES ...

Topz Gospels: Matthew
Topz Gospels: Mark
Topz Gospels: Luke

# Introduction by Paul

God was here before the beginning of anything.

Before the beginning of time.

And Jesus is a part of God. Jesus belongs to God. He *is* God. He goes on forever in both directions – far, far back into the past and way, way forward into the future. *So* far back and *so* far forward, our brains will just never be able to grasp it. Never ever.

John's Gospel is my favourite book of the Bible. I love reading about being with God forever because that's something we can all do! Jesus came to earth to make it happen! All we have to do is believe that He is God's Son and live our lives the way God wants us to. Then that life forever with God – FOREVER! – belongs to us. Not just some time in the future, but now. Right now.

I like to imagine knowing John – the John who wrote John's Gospel. I think about waking up in the morning and going straight round to his house.

I think about him saying, 'Let's go and hang out with Jesus.'

I hear myself ask, 'Can the rest of the Topz Gang come, too?'

'Of course!' John answers.

So we all go with John. We meet up with the rest of Jesus' disciples – and *Him*. Jesus Himself. We listen to Him. We follow Him. We follow Him everywhere!

I can see it all in my head. Can you see it, too? Life with Topz and Jesus? Well, let's imagine it …

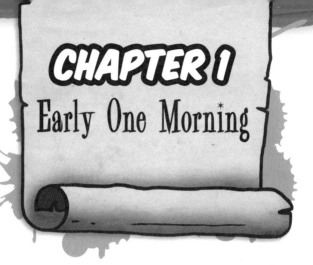

# CHAPTER 1
## Early One Morning

Paul bounces upright. He blinks himself awake. Once. Twice.

Above the horizon, the sky blooms with a peachy glow as the sun begins its steady climb over the sea.

It's early. The rest of the Topz Gang still lie on the beach, sound asleep, around the ashes of last night's campfire. They'd dozed off under the stars. Now the stars have made way for a brand-new day.

Paul blinks again. And again.

'It's all right,' he murmurs. 'It's absolutely all right. I'll just keep blinking until it's absolutely all right …'

He scrunches his eyes tight shut, opens them, scrunches them and opens them again.

Then – 'It's not all right!' he yells. 'It's absolutely not all right! Spots in front of my eyes! Great big blobby spots in front of my eyes! Somebody – anybody – wake up! I've got *spots in front of my eyes*!'

To one side of him, Danny rolls over. His own eyes are bleary. He screws them up.

'What …?' he mumbles. 'What's the … where's the … what's going on …?'

'My eyes!' moans Paul. 'Spots. In front of.'

On the other side of Paul, Benny turns his head.

'What's with all the noise?' he groans. 'I was dreaming. I was having a good dream. You woke me up. Thanks. Thanks a lot.'

By now, Paul is on his feet. He stretches his hands out in front of his face. He peers at them; waggles his fingers.

'Spots,' he whimpers. 'Nothing but spots.'

Sarah drags herself from her sleep and staggers to her feet, too. She stands beside Paul and squints towards his outstretched hands. She glances back towards his face.

'Erm, Paul,' she says. With her wrist, she rubs at an itch on the end of her nose.

'Yes?' whispers Paul, in a voice so small even a gnat would struggle to hear it.

'Paul,' Sarah continues, 'you can see your hands, can't you?'

'Yes.' Again a tiny whisper.

'So, what does that tell you?' Sarah asks.

Paul thinks a moment. 'That they're there?' he suggests hesitantly.

Sarah rolls her still sleepy eyes. 'Yes, but if you can *see* them, what does that mean?'

Once more Paul thinks. Suddenly, his blobby-vision eyes widen.

'Oh! I must be wearing my glasses.' His outstretched hands fly to his mildly surprised face. And, yes, there are his glasses sitting comfortably on his nose.

7

'Yes, Paul,' says Sarah. 'You are wearing your glasses. You must have gone to sleep in your glasses last night. How many times have we told you this is not a good idea? Supposing one of us gets up in the night and trips over you? What happens if a wild animal comes along and *sits on your face*? Seriously, Paul, you have to start taking your glasses off and putting them somewhere safe before you go to sleep at night. At any time in fact.'

'Yes,' Paul nods. 'Yes, you're right. But the blobs, Sarah,' he adds. 'It still doesn't explain the blobs.'

Sarah sighs. 'We're on a beach, Paul. We've been sleeping on a beach. Your glasses are covered in sand!'

Paul stares at her. The spots in front of his eyes make her look strangely blotchy.

Sarah reaches out. Carefully she removes his glasses from his face. Gently, she wipes each lens on her sleeve. She holds them up to her own eyes and peers through them to check they are clean. Then, as carefully as she's taken them off, she slips them back on Paul's bewildered face. He blinks, and blinks again.

'No blobby vision, Paul,' Sarah says. 'Just sand.'

She collapses back down onto her rug and stretches out, arms above her head. Saucy, her cat, who's been asleep on her rug too, opens one indignant eye at the disturbance.

'Crisis over?' mumbles Benny.

'Yup,' Sarah yawns. 'Over and out.'

'Stonking. Can I go back to sleep now?'

'Sleep?' Paul snorts. 'Huh! How can you want to go

back to sleep? Sun's up. It's morning. Just look at the colour of the sky!'

No one looks. At that moment, no one cares.

But Paul looks and keeps on looking. As Topz fall back into silent sleepiness, he wanders down to the water's edge. Miniature waves lap at the shore, trickle back and forth over the gritty sand. Paul stands close enough for them to tickle at his toes, and then splash over his feet.

Red-gold, the sun hangs above the line between sky and sea. The water beneath shimmers under the morning light. It seems to breathe in the colour, soak it up, becoming red-gold itself.

Paul walks. There's no breeze. Nothing to disturb the early stillness. Almost no movement at all, except for Paul himself, who paddles through the shallows, gazing around him at the slowly waking world. A spectacular, mesmerising, *blob-free* world.

He stops a moment. He glances back at the Topz camp. Still no movement there. He shakes his head. They're missing it. They're all missing it. This perfectly peaceful, clear, glowing morning and they're sleeping through it. If they don't get up soon, they'll miss it completely …

Which is when Paul remembers.

He turns. He runs. He's not the fastest runner in the Topz Gang, but he can pelt along at a fair pace when he really puts his mind to it. And his mind is clearly *to it*. In next to no time, he's back up the beach, waving his arms, shouting, 'Hey! *Heeyyy!*'

Sarah sits up with a start. 'What? What is it? Is there a wild animal on my face?' She twists over, horrified. 'Josie, is there? *Is* there? I can't bear to touch it! Is there a wild animal on my face?'

Josie doesn't open her eyes. 'What are you talking about?' she grunts. 'It's just Paul.'

Sarah sighs loudly. 'Oh, will you just lie down and go back to sleep, Paul!'

'No, no!' cries Paul. He begins to jump up and down with excitement. 'Have you forgotten what day it is?'

John slowly props himself up on his elbows. 'We will never forget what day it is,' he grumbles. 'This day will never be forgotten. It's the day *you* won't let us sleep in!' And he flops back down with a grumpy 'Oomph'.

Paul throws up his hands in disbelief. 'But this is the day we *can't* sleep in!' he squeals. 'And when you remember what day it actually is, you won't even *want* to sleep in!'

'Wanna bet?' mutters Dave.

Josie gives up and sits upright on her rug. She rubs at her tired eyes. 'What are you talking about, Paul?' she asks. 'What day is it?'

'The day,' announces Paul, a gleam of triumph lighting his eyes, **'OF THE WEDDING!'**

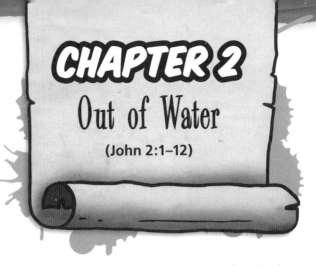

# CHAPTER 2
## Out of Water
**(John 2:1–12)**

Paul sits on the riverbank. He dangles his feet in the water, lifts them out and shakes them off. With the hem of his tunic, he dries between his toes.

'So,' he says, 'how clean do you suppose we should be to go to a wedding?'

'Very clean,' replies Sarah, raking her fingers through her hair, tugging when she meets a tangle.

'Very, very clean,' agrees Josie. 'And it would also help if we didn't look as if we've just spent the night on the beach.'

Benny gives her a sideways glance. 'But we *have* just spent the night on the beach.'

'My point exactly,' says Josie.

Paul stretches his legs out in front of him. 'Who wants to check between my toes?'

'Even for a wedding, Paul,' grins Danny, wrinkling his nose, 'I don't think anyone's going to want to check between your toes.'

The town of Cana where the wedding is to be held isn't far, but the walk to get there is very dusty.

When Topz arrive, Paul gazes down gloomily at his sandalled feet.

'I don't know why I bothered,' he grunts. 'They're filthy. They are honestly and truly completely filthy.'

Sarah shakes her head. 'No one will take any notice of your feet, Paul. This is a wedding. Look at the bride. Just look at her! She's beautiful!'

With wide eyes, the bride gazes at the great crowd of guests who have arrived to share her wedding day. It's as if she can scarcely believe that such a gathering can have anything to do with her.

'That's how I want to look when *I'm* a bride,' says Josie. 'Beautiful like that.'

Benny laughs.

'And why is that funny?' Josie frowns. 'Is it so hard to imagine me looking beautiful?'

'Oh, no, no,' Benny says quickly, 'it's not that. It's just … well, it's just the idea that any of us might get married one day. It's weird.'

'It's hilarious,' giggles Danny.

'Won't make any difference to me,' says Paul. 'I'll still be in the Topz Gang whether I'm married or not.'

With the wedding ceremony over, the festivities begin.

'This must be a very big family,' says John. 'With a *lot* of friends. There are so many people here.'

'And look.' Dave nods his head towards a group of guests who stand a little apart from the rest. They talk and laugh. They look relaxed and happy. **'THERE'S JESUS.'**

'I told you, didn't I?' beams Paul. 'I told you Jesus was going to be here.'

'And not just Jesus, either,' adds Dave. 'There's His mum. Over there. There's Mary.'

The sound of voices and laughter swells. It echoes off the whitewashed walls. It vibrates through the air. And the scents of sweet oils and perfumes and freshly prepared food mingle and rise upwards towards the sky.

It's Sarah who notices Mary step towards Jesus. She nudges Paul. 'Look! Can you hear them? Can you hear what they're saying?'

They edge closer – try, inside their heads, to turn down the hubbub all around them.

'Jesus!' says Mary. 'Oh, Jesus, this isn't good at all. Our hosts – they're running out of wine.'

Dave stands close and listens, too.

'Why does *that* matter?' wonders Sarah. 'Can't they drink something else?'

Dave shakes his head. 'It's not that simple. Not here. If they run out of wine here, it'll make the family look really bad. It could change how people look at them in the town. How people treat them. A wedding celebration here – it's really important to get everything right.'

Jesus looks at His mother a moment. Then, 'You mustn't tell me what to do,' He replies to her gently. 'It's not my time yet.'

Even so, Mary bustles away to find the servants and tells them to do whatever Jesus says.

Shortly afterwards, Topz see Jesus make His way towards the servants, too.

'You see these?' Jesus says to them.

He points to six large stone jars.

'Fill them up with water,' Jesus tells the servants. 'Right to the brim.'

The servants do as He says. It takes some time. The jars hold a lot of water.

'Good,' smiles Jesus when they've finished. 'Now, take a cupful of that water to the man who's organising the party.'

'It's just water,' whispers Sarah. 'It's not water they're running out of. It's wine.'

From the looks on their faces, the servants have the same thought. They glance uncertainly at each other. Mary has told them to do as Jesus says, but does this Man really know what's going on? Has He understood the problem?

'Erm ...' One of the servants stands in front of the party organiser. He holds out a cup of water from one of the jars. 'I've been told to bring this to you ...'

The organiser glances at him; glances at the cup. He takes it. He lifts it to his lips and sips. He looks again at the servant – and his eyes light up.

Then he calls to the bridegroom: 'First time I've known this to happen. Everyone always serves the best wine at the start of the feast and then brings out the cheap wine once the guests have already had plenty to drink. But you?' he laughs. 'You've kept the best wine for now!'

The servant, his brow furrowed in confusion, gives a little nod to the party organiser and hurries back to the stone jars.

None of them are filled with water anymore. They all brim with more than enough wine to see the feast through to its end.

And his jaw drops in complete astonishment.

Sarah shakes her head. 'That's not possible. It's not possible! It was water. I saw the servants fill the jars up with water. How can it be wine now?'

Sarah gazes across at Jesus. He stands and talks with His disciples; talks with other wedding guests. He behaves as though nothing has happened.

'But if Jesus is going to work a miracle,' she says, 'shouldn't it be for something really, *really* important?'

'This *is* really important,' Dave answers. 'It might not seem it to us but it really is here. It's so important to this wedding family and to how the people of the town see them that this day is successful. It's all about their position in their society. And don't you see what Jesus has done?' Dave goes on. 'He's worked a miracle that shows He's interested in our *ordinary* problems – our day-to-day stuff. He's shown that He cares about everything in our lives! Big *and* not so big.

'More than that, by making sure the wine doesn't run out, Jesus has sorted out a tricky situation. **HE'S SEEN A NEED – AND HE'S FILLED IT.**'

Slowly, Sarah nods. 'Which is why He's here, isn't it?' she says. 'Why He's on earth. To fill *our* need. We need God so Jesus has come to tell us, come to show us, how to reach Him. And how to let Him reach us.'

She glances back towards the stone jars – the jars now holding miracle wine, not water.

'That wine will run out in the end, won't it?' she adds. 'But the life God wants to give us – the life that Jesus wants us to have – that'll never run out. It's forever.'

*'in Cana in Galilee … [Jesus] revealed his glory'* (John 2:11)

16

# CHAPTER 3
## So Much
### (John 3:1–21)

Paul stifles a yawn. Unsuccessfully.

Danny glances at him. 'We should head out to the fields. Find somewhere to camp for the night.'

'No!' Paul shakes his head vigorously. 'I'm not even tired. Anyway, it's early.'

'It's not early,' answers Danny. 'It's been dark for ages. I don't know about anyone else but I'm worn out and you're dead beat. We should go now.'

Paul sighs. 'But Jesus is just over there. Can't we stay a bit longer? At least until *He* goes to bed?'

'Danny's right,' says Josie. 'We should probably go.' She clambers to her feet. 'We can find Jesus again tomorrow.'

Once more, Paul sighs. Louder this time.

'Fine,' he grunts. He stands up and stretches. 'But – and I'm sorry but I have to say this – sometimes you Topz act like you're my … *parents* …'

The night is cool. Overhead, a deep blue-black sky glistens with stars. Every now and then, a thin rag of cloud covers the half-moon. Then it drifts on past, and the silver shimmer of moonlight can once more trickle downwards, uninterrupted.

Topz step out of the alleyway where they've been sitting – and a man almost barges straight into them. In his hurry, he barely hesitates. He doesn't apologise. He just swerves sideways and scurries on past.

The Gang turn. At the far end of the alley, they can still see Jesus. And then the hurrying man suddenly emerges from the shadows and marches right up to Him. He must have known exactly where to find Him.

Paul frowns. 'Who is he?'

'He's a Pharisee,' mutters Benny. He watches the man suspiciously. 'He's a teacher. I think his name's Nicodemus.'

'Bit late to be out looking for Jesus,' says John.

Benny shrugs. 'Like I say, he's a Pharisee. His rules for life don't fit in with what Jesus teaches. Maybe he doesn't want to be seen talking to Him.'

Nicodemus speaks.

'Teacher,' he says to Jesus, 'we know that God has sent You. God is with You – He must be. Otherwise You would never be able to work the miracles we have seen.'

'Let me tell you the truth,' Jesus answers. 'If anyone wants to see God's kingdom, they must be born again.'

Nicodemus stares into Jesus' face, flecked with shadow under the moon. He's puzzled. 'But that can never happen,' he murmurs. 'How is it possible for a person to be back inside their mother and then be born for a second time?'

'No,' says Jesus, 'that's not what I mean. Someone is born into the world through their parents here on earth.

But to see God's kingdom – to live with God forever – you need a *spiritual* birth. Everyone must be born again like that.'

Again, Nicodemus looks confused.

'God's Spirit – the Holy Spirit – is like the wind,' Jesus explains. 'You can hear the sound of the wind. You can't see it but you can hear it and feel it, and you can watch it move what it touches. Just like that, the Holy Spirit can't be seen. You'll never know who He's going to touch next, but He will lead people to find God. He leads people to their spiritual birth.'

Nicodemus looks even more confused. 'I don't understand this. How can it be?'

Jesus stares at him. 'And how can you not know these things?' He asks. 'You are a teacher – an important teacher. I know all this. I'm telling you what I know, but none of you will believe me! How can I get you to believe what I say about God's kingdom in heaven? The Son of Man has come down from there, and the Son of Man will be lifted up again. And everyone who believes in Him will be able to spend forever with their Father God.

'Are you hearing me?' Jesus says. 'God loves the world so much that He has given up His only Son, so that every single person who believes in Him will never have to die. Because God will give them a life with Him that will never end.

'God hasn't sent His Son to look down His nose at people and give them a good telling off for all the things they do wrong! For all the ways they don't live how God wants them to.

'God has sent His Son as a way for Him to forgive them.

'As a way for Him to save the whole world.'

Jesus pauses. There's a lot to take in, so much in what He says, He knows that.

'Those who believe that I am God's Son,' He continues gently, 'will not be judged by God. But God has already judged those who don't believe.

'The Son is a light that has come into this world. But people who do wrong things – who want to go on doing wrong things – they stay away from that light. They hate it. They want to stay hidden in darkness so that the wrong things they do won't be seen.

'It's those who obey God – who love Him and want to live their lives the way He asks them to – it's those people who hurry to the light. They shine with the light! And everyone can see that they are God's friends.'

'So, let me get this straight,' Paul mutters. 'I've been born again, haven't I? We all have. Haven't we?'

'Yes, we have,' answers Dave. 'We were all born again the moment we believed that Jesus is the Son of God and asked Him to come into our lives. The minute we told God we were sorry for the things we've done wrong and asked Him to forgive us. Because as soon as we did all that, the Holy Spirit came to live inside us.'

'Huh!' smiles Paul. 'So when that happened we were born the second time. And that was the spiritual birth.'

'I think I'd like that on a t-shirt,' grins Benny.

## '"BORN TWICE!"'

Josie looks past Paul to Jesus. There's no sign of

Nicodemus now. He's gone. He hasn't passed them again. Perhaps he's left the other way.

'But how has God given up His Son?' she asks. 'How is sending Jesus to earth giving Him up?'

Sarah turns towards her friend. 'We're in the middle of Jesus' story. We haven't seen everything happen yet.' She speaks quietly. 'But I know this and so do you: God is holy. Completely holy. He never does wrong, He can't bear it. And because He is holy, He has to punish the people He loves for the wrong things *they* do. But by sending Jesus,' Sarah says, 'God's found a way not to have to punish us.'

Josie looks at Sarah; searches her face.

'God's giving up His Son,' Sarah ends slowly, 'because Jesus is going to take the punishment instead.'

*'For God loved the world so much that he gave his only Son, so that everyone who believes in him may not die but have eternal life.' (John 3:16)*

# CHAPTER 4
## The Woman at the Well
### (John 4:5–28)

'I like it here,' says John. 'I wonder why Jewish people don't.'

Jesus is making another journey. One that has taken Him into Samaria and a town there called Sychar. His disciples travel with Him. Topz follow after them.

'It's not Samaria the Jews don't like,' says Danny. 'Jews and Samaritans just don't get on with each other. They believe different things. About God and about how to serve Him and worship Him. So they don't mix.'

'Jesus mixes with everyone, though, doesn't He?' says John. 'Because Jesus knows that everyone needs God.'

Up ahead of them, Topz watch as the disciples leave Jesus at a well to go into the town and buy food.

Jesus sits down. The journey has been a very long one. He must be worn out. Topz certainly are.

They see a woman approach Him. A Samaritan woman. At least, she walks, carrying a stone jar, towards the well to draw out some water. Perhaps she's not aware of Jesus sitting there.

Jesus doesn't move. He stays where He is. He waits until she is close enough to speak to.

**'MAY I HAVE SOME WATER, PLEASE?'** He asks.

'Like I say,' says John to the rest of the Gang. 'Jesus mixes with everyone.'

The woman is startled, shocked to have been spoken to at all, let alone by this Jewish Man.

She stands still uncomfortably. She hardly looks Him in the eye.

'How can You ask me for a drink of water?' she asks finally. Hesitantly. She knows that Jews have nothing to do with Samaritans. Jews even refuse to use cups and bowls that Samaritan people have used. 'I am a Samaritan,' she says. 'You are a Jew. How can You ask me this?'

Jesus smiles. A kind smile that chases the tired lines from His face.

'You don't know what God wants to give you, do you?' He says. 'You don't realise who it is who asks you for a drink. If you did, you would ask *Him* for water and He would give you water that would bring you life.'

The woman shakes her head. Whoever this Man is, what He says doesn't seem to make sense.

'But, Sir,' she answers, 'this well is very deep. And You don't even have a bucket with You. Where are You going to draw this life-giving water from?'

Again, Jesus smiles. His eyes glow with warmth.

'Anyone who drinks the water from this well will be thirsty again,' He tells her. 'But people who drink the water that I can give to them – they won't be thirsty anymore. That water will become a spring inside them.

A spring that will lead them to live with God. Not just for a little while but for always.'

John listens intently to Jesus' words.

'He's talking about the Holy Spirit again,' he whispers. 'Just like He did with Nicodemus. The water is the Spirit. That's what Jesus means. And if we ask Him for that water – the water that brings life – then the Spirit will come and live inside us, and we'll never have to be without God. Our lives will go on with Him forever!'

Paul nods his head. 'Jesus is giving that woman the chance to know God. To be God's friend. I wonder if she'll take it ...'

Topz wait. They watch.

They see the woman lift her eyes and begin to gaze at Jesus. Full in the face. They see her lower the stone jar from her shoulder and stand it on the ground beside the well.

They hear her say: 'Oh, please, Sir, please give me the water You're talking about. Then I won't be thirsty ever again. And I won't have to come back here to draw water from this well.'

She still hasn't quite understood what Jesus is saying. Not completely.

'Go and get your husband,' Jesus says. 'Then come back here with him.'

Instantly, the woman drops her gaze. Once again, she seems to find it hard to look at Him.

'I don't have a husband.' She speaks so quietly, Topz almost can't catch the words.

Jesus nods. 'That's true. You've been married to five men, and the man you live with at the moment, he isn't really your husband. Is he?'

The woman's eyes open wide at this. How can this Man know? How can He possibly know? They've never met before.

'I can see …' she murmurs, 'I can see that You must be a prophet.'

Sarah glances at her friends. 'Why doesn't Jesus tell her who He is? If He tells her, she'll understand.'

'She'll only understand if she believes Him,' says Dave.

'You are a Samaritan,' Jesus says. 'You haven't really discovered who God is. Not yet. But one day, people will be so full of God's Spirit that they will know exactly who He is. They will praise Him for exactly who He is!

'God's Spirit is powerful. Only God's Spirit can teach people to really praise God and to know Him.'

'But I do know,' the woman replies, 'I do know that the Messiah will come one day. He will come to us and He will tell us everything we need to know.'

Sarah holds her breath. Will He tell her? Will Jesus tell her who He is now?

**'THAT'S ME,'** Jesus says. Gently. Simply. 'I am talking to you and that is who I am.'

The woman's hands fly to her mouth. She gasps. Can she believe Him?

But how can she *not* believe Him?

'Jesus! We have food!' The shout interrupts them.

The woman turns abruptly. A group of men walk towards them. Jesus' disciples. They have come back from the town with something to eat.

She looks again at Jesus, but doesn't speak. She just hurries away, not even picking up her water jar to take with her.

# CHAPTER 5
## Who He Is
### (John 4:29–30,39–42)

The woman moves fast: half trotting, half walking. Topz have to jog to keep up. John's dog, Gruff, bounces along beside him, glad of the chance of a good run.

Is the woman scared of Jesus? Is that why she's left in such a hurry?

She reaches the edge of the town. As she sees people in the streets, she scurries up to them.

'Come with me!' she gabbles. 'Come with me and see this amazing Man I've just met! Do you know what He did? He told me all the things I've done. He knew all about me. He says He's the Messiah. Can you believe it? He says He's the Messiah and – well – He could be. I honestly do believe He *could* be!'

The people she talks to are curious at first, and then excited. The ones who know the woman have never seen her so radiant before. They stop what they're doing and head off with her to find the Man she talks about.

Topz make their way back through the streets too, in amongst the steady stream of people who now walk out to the well. To where Jesus still sits. There, the Samaritans crowd around Him. And they believe in Him because of what the woman has told them about Him! They're so excited to talk to Him and to listen to Him that they even invite Him to stay with them.

So Jesus stays in Sychar for two more days. He speaks to the Samaritans there. He teaches them. And as more and more people hear Him, they realise who He is. Who He *must be*. And they believe in Him.

They trust Him.

Sarah sits on the edge of a group of Jesus' listeners, Saucy snuggled into her lap. She watches the faces of the people around her as they soak up His words. As their eyes glow with wonder and astonishment that this Man – the Man whom God has sent, His very own Son – should choose to spend time with them, should want to talk to them.

'God really does love every single person on the planet,' Sarah says. 'He wants them all to know who He is and how they can share their lives with Him.'

'It's a big job, though,' answers Josie. 'Letting everyone know. It's a huge job.'

Sarah smiles. 'But Jesus has started it off for us. **HE'S SHOWING US WHAT TO DO.** Jesus doesn't just tell some people and not others. He doesn't pick and choose. He tells *everyone He meets*.

'Because God has a new life for all of us. And He wants to make sure we all know about it.'

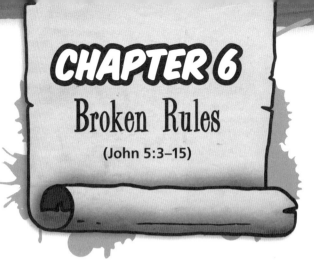

# CHAPTER 6
## Broken Rules
### (John 5:3–15)

'I wonder what it's like to be famous?' says Paul.

Gruff trots along ahead of the Gang as they follow the road Jesus has taken. It's quiet out – a rest day. The Sabbath day. Paul watches the scruffy little dog stop and shove his nose into a tuft of grass.

'Gruff does a lot of sniffing, doesn't he?' he adds.

John shrugs. 'It's what dogs do.'

'Not sure I'd like it,' says Benny.

'What? Sniffing?' asks Paul.

'No! Being famous.'

'Oh. Why not?'

'Well, think about it. You could never go out, for a start. Well, you could, but people would keep coming up to you and asking for your autograph or something. And you'd never be able to just hang around on the beach and kick a ball about because your "fans" would want to talk to you all the time. And if you didn't go out, they'd probably find out where you live and camp outside your house. They'd never leave you alone. I couldn't stick it.'

Paul nods. 'Don't panic, Benny,' he says. 'I don't think it's something you're ever likely to have to worry about.'

'Meaning what?' Benny frowns.

'I just can't ever imagine you having "fans",' says Paul.

Benny's frown sinks deeper into his forehead. 'And why not?'

'Oh, I don't mean it in a bad way. I just mean it's hard to imagine your friends being famous. Can you imagine *me* being famous?'

'We *might* be famous,' says Danny. 'One day.'

Sarah lets Saucy jump down from her arms. The fluffy bundle lands lightly. Even so, as her paws hit the parched road, they create a mini dust explosion. She stalks towards Gruff – gingerly inspects the grass where he's buried his nose. Then she sits, uninterested and begins to wash.

Sarah watches her, a half smile lighting her face. 'Imagine being famous like Jesus. People hear of Him. People can't wait to meet Him. But lots of them don't even know what He looks like.'

'Like the woman in Samaria,' says Josie. 'She was talking to Jesus and she had no idea. But she knew *about* Him. She knew she was waiting for Him.'

Dave stands in the middle of the road. He can see people up ahead of them. A lot of people. Jesus walks towards them.

'The trouble with being famous like Jesus,' he says quietly, 'is that, yes, you have fans – but you're going to end up with enemies, too.'

He turns to the Gang. 'We should go. Catch up.'

As Topz get closer, they see that this crowd of people, for once, aren't actually waiting for Jesus.

They are ill or disabled. Some of them can't see. Some can't walk. Some can barely move at all.

They sit and lie around a pool. A pool of water that, every now and again, God fills with His Spirit. At that moment, when the water's full of God, if a sick person steps or is lifted into it, they are made well.

One man lies a little way from the pool. He is very thin. He looks sad and lonely. As if he's been sick for years. As if he can't even remember what it's like to be able to move.

This is the man Jesus talks to.

'You have been ill for so long,' He says to him. 'Don't you want to get better?'

The man lifts his eyes to Jesus. One half of him is surprised that a passer-by has spoken to him. The other half seems too tired to care.

'There is no one here to help me into the water at the right time,' he mumbles. 'I try but … there is always someone who is quicker than I am.'

Jesus watches him. He sees the dullness in the man's eyes; the sadness in his face. Jesus feels sad Himself.

'Stand up,' He says. 'Stand up now, pick up the mat you lie on, and walk.'

The man stares at Him.

A moment passes. Then … What's going on …?

Almost as soon as Jesus has spoken, he feels different. He barely even thinks about what he's doing.

He just follows Jesus' instructions because somehow – miraculously – he knows he can.

He senses the rush of energy as he pushes down onto his feet and stands. For the first time in years. He feels the strength in his spine as he twists and bends to pick up his mat. He feels his heart pound as his legs begin to move.

He can walk! This Stranger has spoken to him, and he can walk!

There's a murmur among the people who can see. How can this be? What is it they've just watched happen? Is it real? Will it last?

'It's a miracle,' grins Benny. **'A STONKING MIRACLE!'**

With his mat rolled up in his hand, the man Jesus has made better walks through the crowd at the pool. Is he dreaming? If he is, this dream is more real, more extraordinary than any he has ever had before.

Suddenly – 'You there!'

The shout is stern. Harsh. The man looks towards the person who has barked at him. Some Pharisees stand and stare at him.

The same voice barks again: 'Have you forgotten what day it is? Today is the Sabbath. There are many things you must not do on the Sabbath day. It is against our Law. Carrying your mat is one of them, you must know that.'

Benny shakes his head. 'I don't get these rules. How can carrying a mat be against the Law?'

'The Pharisees think of carrying anything as work,' whispers Dave. He doesn't want them to hear him. 'And on the Sabbath day no one is supposed to do any work at all.'

The man answers the Pharisee with the barky voice. 'There was a Man, and He made me better. He's the one who told me to pick up my mat and walk.'

The Pharisee's eyes grow dark. 'What Man? Who is He?'

Topz follow the healed man's eyes as he looks around him, searching for Jesus. The man doesn't know who He is, and now he can't find Him.

There are so many other people there and Jesus has managed to slip away.

'I don't know,' the man shrugs. 'I don't know where He is.'

The Gang aren't sure where Jesus has gone either. They didn't notice Him leave. It's the sick man who's well again that they've been watching; that everyone has been watching.

But they find Him later. And Jesus has found the man He's healed again, too.

'You have your life back now,' Jesus says. 'A life to live because you are better. So stop doing wrong things with it. Don't make God unhappy.'

The man stares at Jesus. But he doesn't thank Him. He doesn't even speak to Him.

Instead he turns away, and sidles off to find the Pharisees.

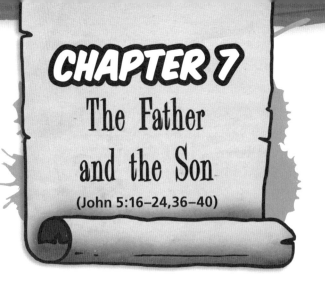

# CHAPTER 7

## The Father and the Son

(John 5:16–24,36–40)

Josie scowls. 'Where's that man going? Can you believe that? Jesus made him better and he didn't even say thank You.'

'Jesus did more than make him better,' grunts John. 'He gave him his life back.'

They watch the man as he slinks past them. They see him head straight towards a group of Pharisees. One of them is the Pharisee with the loud voice, who told him off earlier for carrying his mat.

'It's Jesus,' says the man. 'Jesus is the one who healed me. He's the one who told me to pick up my mat.'

'Why's he done that?' cries Sarah. 'Why would he give Jesus away?'

Dave makes a face. 'More to the point … what are the Pharisees going to do about it?'

The Pharisees waste no time. They march up to Jesus, their mouths set in hard, angry lines, their shoulders pushed back.

'What's the meaning of this, Jesus?' They spit His name out of their mouths as if it tastes nasty. 'How dare You? How dare You tell someone to carry his mat on the Sabbath day! And how dare You heal someone on the Sabbath day! It is against our Law to do any kind of work. Why must You go against our Law?'

Jesus doesn't seem surprised to see them. He doesn't even raise an eyebrow at their complaints.

'My Father never stops working,' He says. 'I must get on with my work, too.'

Dave sees the spark of hate flash in the Pharisees' eyes. Their mouths twist. Their teeth clench. Who does this Man think He is? He stands in front of them, so calm, so cool. But He has just called God, His Father. *His own Father*! This Man has said that He is the same as God!

Jesus knows what's in their minds. Every thought.

Jesus knows everything about them.

'Listen to me,' He says, 'because this is the truth. The Son can't do anything by Himself. He can only do what He sees His Father doing. And He does what His Father does.

'You see, the Father loves His Son and lets Him know everything that He's doing. And He wants His Son to do even more incredible things than making the man at the pool better. You'll be astonished!'

Jesus stares at the men in front of Him. He longs for them to understand.

But He knows they never will.

'The Father can bring those who have died back to life,' He says. 'And the Son can give life to whoever He chooses, exactly like that.

'Can't you understand?' Jesus adds. 'How can anyone say they respect the Father if they don't respect the Son He sent?

'What I'm saying is true: people who believe what I say, and believe in my Father who sent me – they will have life that lasts forever. They will not be judged. They are already living that forever life with God.'

Dave sees the hardness in the Pharisees' faces. He doesn't like the way they look at Jesus with curled lips and scornful eyes.

### THEY LISTEN TO HIM BUT THEY DON'T HEAR HIM.

They gaze at Him but they don't *really see* Him because they don't believe who He is. They don't believe that He is God's Son.

So God won't be able to give them that life with Him that lasts forever.

The Pharisees make Dave feel angry. But he knows that's not the way Jesus feels about them.

He knows the Pharisees make Jesus sad.

'Everything I do,' Jesus says to them, 'all the things my Father has given me to do – those things are your proof! They *prove* that the Father has sent me.

'And the Father tells you this, too. But you don't know His voice and you can't see His face and you don't hold on to what He teaches you! Because you won't believe that I am the One He has sent to you!

'Oh, yes, you study the Scriptures,' Jesus continues, 'because you think that they hold the secret of a never-ending life. But these Scriptures you read, these writings, they talk about *me* – and you still won't come to me! You won't come to me so that I can give you the life with God that you're searching for.'

Topz wander away.

There's no sign of the man Jesus healed now. Perhaps he's gone home. Perhaps right at this moment, his family are clapping their hands to their mouths and jumping up and down with excitement when they see him. Perhaps the man himself still thinks it might all be a dream.

Whatever he's doing right now, Dave wonders – now that he can walk and run and work and live his life again – will even he believe that Jesus is God's Son?

38

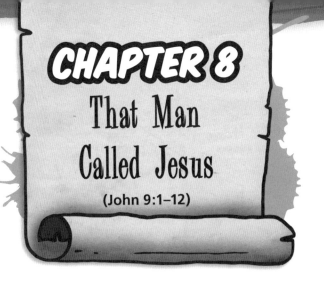

# CHAPTER 8
## That Man Called Jesus
### (John 9:1–12)

Paul sits with his back against a wall. He munches on a bread roll and balances a second bread roll on the top of his head.

Josie rounds the street corner and spots him.

'Erm …' She blinks at him. 'What are you doing with that bread roll?'

Paul blinks back at her. As if the answer's obvious. 'I'm eating it. What does it look like?'

'No, not *that* one,' says Josie. 'The other one. The one on your head.'

'Oh, yeah!' Paul throws up a hand to check it's still there, even though it obviously is. 'Benny put it there.'

Josie frowns. 'Benny put a bread roll on your head?'

'Yup,' nods Paul.

Josie folds her arms. 'I refer you to my earlier question,' she says. 'What are you doing with it?'

'It's an experiment,' answers Paul. 'To see how long it takes for a bird to swoop down and snatch it.'

'I see.' Josie unfolds her arms and puts her hands on her hips. 'So how long have you been sitting there?'

'Not sure. About an hour ... probably. Could be longer. You see, I think the problem is my glasses,' he adds. 'I reckon they're putting the birds off.'

'How's that?'

'Because they flash,' he says. 'Not on their own, that'd be weird. But they flash when the sun hits them. Birds might be put off by flashy things.'

Josie presses her lips together. 'And where do you think Benny is?' she asks.

'He's in the next street along. He's sitting there with a bread roll on his head, too. You see, it was sort of a race,' Paul explains. 'You know – whose head will the bread roll get nabbed from by a bird first? That sort of thing.'

'That sort of thing, right,' nods Josie.

'Only Benny can't be doing any better than I am, because he hasn't turned up yet.'

'So,' says Josie, 'if I was to tell you that I've just left Benny, not sitting in the next street with a bread roll on his head, but playing hopscotch with the rest of Topz – would that surprise you?'

Paul's eyes narrow.

'A bit ... A lot ... Playing hopscotch ...?'

'That's why I came to find you,' says Josie. 'I know you hate hopscotch so I thought you might want to do something else.'

'Right,' says Paul. 'Thanks.'

There's a pause. Then Paul gets to his feet.

'Erm …' says Josie. 'You might want to take the bread roll off your head now.'

Paul reaches up to grab it. Then he brings it straight to his mouth and takes a big bite.

Josie wrinkles her nose. 'Eew! You're not seriously going to eat that, are you? It's been in your hair!'

'It's *my* hair,' Paul shrugs. 'Anyway, waste not, want not, isn't that what they say?'

'Well, yeah, but I'm not sure it applies to food that's been in your hair.'

'Oh, it's fine,' Paul replies. 'I've done it before.'

Josie and Paul turn out of the side street where Paul has been sitting. Almost at once, Josie stops.

'There's Jesus.'

Jesus stands with His disciples looking down at a beggar man who is blind and sits at the side of the road.

One of the disciples whispers to Jesus. 'Is it because he has done wrong things that he's blind?' he asks. 'Or is it because his parents have done wrong things?'

Jesus shakes His head. 'That has nothing to do with it,' He answers. 'This man isn't blind because of what he or his parents have done.

'But God does want to show His power through this blindness. We must keep on doing God's work while there's daylight. Because when night comes, no one will be able to work. As long as I am in the world, I am the light of the world.'

Jesus crouches down. He spits into the dust under His feet to mix up a tiny bit of mud.

Paul peers hard. 'Did Jesus just do what I think He did?'

'Yes.' Josie stares. 'Yes, He did.'

Gently, Jesus rubs the mud onto the blind man's eyes.

'Now,' He says, 'you know how to find your way to the Pool of Siloam? Go there and wash your face in the water.'

Josie and Paul watch the man. He walks a little hesitantly. But this is his home. He can't see it but he knows it very well. And he knows exactly how to get to the Pool.

'Why doesn't Jesus go with him?' Paul wonders.

Josie smiles. 'Because He knows what's going to happen. He said it, didn't He? He's the light of the world. He opens people's eyes so that they can see through the darkness and find God. And He'll open this man's eyes so that he can see the world all around him.'

They follow the man. They see him crouch by the water and wash his face, just as Jesus has told him to.

They watch him blink and screw up his eyes as, suddenly, he can see; he's dazzled by the daylight.

And as he walks back the way he has come, people who know him, people who recognise him as the blind beggar man, can't believe their *own* eyes.

'Isn't that … *him?*'

'It is! I do believe it is!'

'No, it can't be. It's just someone who looks like him.'

But the man, with the biggest smile ever to have brightened his face, splutters, 'It is me. It *is me!*'

What's happened is amazing. Incredible!

But Josie is suddenly worried. 'Will he tell them about Jesus? If he does, Jesus will be in trouble again. It's the Sabbath day today, isn't it? The Pharisees will be angry.'

'Jesus won't care,' Paul replies. 'This is what He came to earth to do: show people God.'

'How can you see?' asks a woman. 'You were blind. How can you now see?'

The man looks at her; stares at her. He takes in every detail of her face. The colour of her eyes, the colour of her hair. At last he can see the people who speak to him!

'It was that Man,' he says. 'That Man called Jesus.

## *IT WAS HIM WHO MADE ME SEE.*'

'Well, where is He?' asks the woman.

All the people there want to know where He is.

The man shakes his head. He shrugs his shoulders.

'I don't know.'

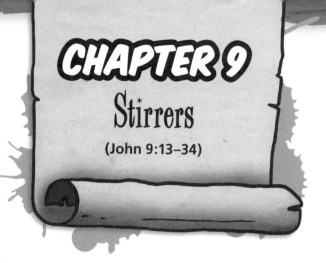

# CHAPTER 9

## Stirrers

**(John 9:13–34)**

'Where are we going?' asks John.

He keeps a close eye on Gruff. Topz are part of a small crowd of people bustling through the streets. He doesn't want to lose sight of his dog in amongst the hurrying feet and flapping tunics.

'I told you,' says Josie. 'We're following that man up the front.'

The man up the front is the man whose eyes Jesus has healed. The crowd hustles him along.

'Yes, but why?' Sarah wants to know.

'Because Jesus made him better,' says Paul. 'And these people all around us – they're taking him to the Pharisees.'

As he stands in front of them, the man who was blind explains to the Pharisees how it is that he can now see.

'Jesus,' Sarah murmurs. 'The Man God sent. Don't they get it?'

'This … *thing* … has happened on the Sabbath day,' says one of the Pharisees. He eyes the man closely. Suspiciously. 'Jesus claims that God has sent Him here.

Only God can't have sent Him because He does work on the Sabbath. He doesn't obey the Sabbath Law.'

But instead of all the others in the group agreeing, for once some of the Pharisees don't seem so sure.

'Are you trying to tell us,' says one of them, 'that a man who doesn't obey God – who actively goes *against* God – could work miracles like this?'

Josie gives Sarah a nudge. Her eyes sparkle. 'Look at that! Even some of the Pharisees are beginning to wonder about Jesus now!'

'So,' another of them asks, taking a step towards the man, 'you say it was Jesus who got rid of your blindness. Well, who do you think He is?'

The man doesn't hesitate. He looks the Pharisee straight in the eye. 'He is a prophet,' he says.

'No!' hisses Benny. 'He's met Jesus and he's still got it wrong.'

'He's got a bit of it right,' whispers Dave. 'Prophets are sent by God to speak for Him. So if he thinks Jesus is a prophet, he must believe God sent Him.'

The Pharisees mutter amongst themselves.

At last, one of them – one of those who doesn't want to believe Jesus is who He says He is – announces, 'Of course, this could all be a trick. Perhaps this man was never blind at all.'

Josie's jaw drops. 'One thing's for sure,' she mutters, 'he was never as blind as those Pharisees are.'

The Pharisees won't leave it alone. There's hate inside them: hate for Jesus. It's growing. And **THEY WANT TO STIR UP HATE IN OTHER PEOPLE**, too.

They demand to see the man's parents.

'Is this man your son?' they ask them. 'Apparently, he's been blind ever since he was born. So tell us – how come he can see now?'

The man's parents fidget. They look uneasy. Even frightened. They know what important people the Pharisees are. They know they have power.

And they don't want to get into trouble.

The Pharisees have made it very clear that anyone who believes Jesus is God's Son will never again be allowed to go into a synagogue to worship God.

'Tell them,' whispers Paul. 'Just tell them the truth.'

At last, the man's parents speak. 'This is our son, and yes, when he was born he was blind. But we know no more than you. We don't know how he can see now, and we certainly don't know who made him better. Anyway, why are you asking us about this? He's a grown man, isn't he? Ask *him*. He can speak for himself.'

Paul shakes his head. 'How can they do that? Jesus has healed their son. Why can't they stand up for Him?'

Josie shrugs. She gazes with sad eyes at the man's parents. 'Maybe it's just not that easy,' she answers. 'Look at them. I think they're really scared.'

The Pharisees do speak to the man again.

And the man doesn't seem nearly as frightened as his parents are.

'I don't know anything about the Man I met,' he says. 'All I know is that I was blind – and now I can see.'

'But how did He do it?' the Pharisees insist. 'Come on, tell us the truth.'

Frustrated, the man rolls his brand-new eyes. 'I *have* told you the truth!' he answers. 'Why do you want me to keep going over this? Perhaps you'd really like to be His disciples, too!'

The Pharisees' faces cloud with fury. 'How dare you!' one of them scowls. 'We don't even know where this Man comes from!'

'Well, isn't that an odd thing?' says the man in front of them. 'You say you don't know where He comes from, but He made my eyes see again.

'If anyone goes against God, does God listen to them and do as they say? Of course He doesn't! We know that. But God does listen to people who obey Him. To the people who respect Him. He *does* do what those people ask Him to do.'

The man pauses a moment. Are these Pharisees really so ... *blind?*

'Ever since the beginning of time,' he finishes quietly, 'has anyone ever heard of someone curing a person who was born blind? No! If the Man who gave me my sight hadn't come from God, He would never have been able to do this.'

The Pharisees, the ones who want to hush up all this talk of Jesus – they ban the man from the synagogue. He's not allowed to worship God there again.

# CHAPTER 10
## Shepherd Man
### (John 9:35–41; 10:1–21)

Topz don't know where he's gone. The man whose eyes Jesus has made better.

They only find him again when they find Jesus. Because Jesus has been looking for him, too.

And there are Pharisees around. They watch the man closely. They watch Jesus.

Jesus steps up to the man and asks him, 'Do you believe in the Son of Man?'

'If You tell me who He is,' the man answers, 'then I will believe in Him.'

'He still doesn't know,' murmurs Josie. 'How can he still not know?'

Jesus smiles. 'But you have already met Him. He is talking to you right now.'

The man sucks in a great gasp of air. He falls onto his knees in front of Jesus.

'Oh, Lord!' he cries. 'I believe!'

Jesus watches him. 'I have come here,' He says, 'so that those who are blind will see.'

'To open people's eyes,' Josie murmurs.

'So that people who can't see God – who don't understand how to make friends with Him – will find Him.'

'But there are those who think they know God,' Jesus continues, 'who can't see Him at all.'

The Pharisees instantly butt in.

'What do you mean?' one of them asks. 'Are you trying to say that we're blind to God?'

Jesus falls quiet for a moment. Then He answers, 'If you really couldn't see God, if you *knew* that you couldn't see Him – then I could help you. But you believe that you *can* see Him. You believe you have the answers to "knowing God" without listening to me. Without recognising me. So ...' and Jesus shakes His head. 'So, I can't help you.'

Danny shivers. A sudden prickle of fear creeps over him. Through him.

'That can't be right.' He stares round at his friends. 'That's not right, Jesus can help everyone.'

Sarah gives a little shake of her head. 'The trouble is, Danny,' she whispers, 'not everyone wants to be helped ...'

'This is the truth, then,' Jesus says. He faces the Pharisees. He faces towards everyone who listens. 'Anyone who tries to get into a sheep pen without using the gate – that person is a thief. A robber.

'Only the man who walks into the sheep pen through the gate is the shepherd. And when the sheep hear the shepherd's voice calling to them, they let him lead them out of the pen. They let him lead them because he knows them. He calls to each one of them. He uses their names.

'And the sheep know their shepherd's voice, so they follow him. He walks ahead of them, and they follow after him.

'Now,' Jesus says, and His voice warms as He tells His story, 'would they follow just anyone? No! Of course, they wouldn't! They would run away from someone else because they wouldn't know that person's voice.'

The Pharisees glance at each other. They don't understand. They can see the confusion on each other's faces, but they'll never admit it.

Jesus knows how they feel.

'What I'm telling you is the truth,' He says again. 'I am the gate to the sheep pen. The gate for the sheep – that is, my people, the ones God has given to me. The sheep didn't listen to anyone who came before me, because anyone else is a thief. A robber.

'I say it again, *I am the gate*. Whoever comes to God *through me*, the gate, will be saved for God – will have a life forever with God.

'Thieves only want to steal. To take away! **I HAVE COME TO GIVE LIFE.** To give more life than you could ever imagine.'

'Jesus is the only way to God,' Sarah whispers. 'That's why He's the gate. If we don't believe in Jesus – really, totally believe in Jesus – then we won't have the life He talks about.'

'That's why He says He can't help some of the Pharisees,' says Dave. 'Because they won't believe in Him. They think they can earn their place with God by making their own rules and following them.'

'I am also the good shepherd,' Jesus goes on.
'A shepherd will do anything to protect his sheep, won't
he?' He says. 'But if someone else is paid to look after
the sheep, that person will never care for them as much
the shepherd does. If he sees a wolf coming, he'll run
away. So the wolf will be able to steal a sheep or two,
and chase the others in all directions.

'Well, I am the good shepherd and I'm ready to die for my sheep.

'I know my sheep, and they know me as well as my Father and I know each other. And there are more of my sheep out there, too, who aren't in the pen yet. They will listen to my voice and I must lead them in.'

Jesus scans the faces of His listeners. He knows which ones start to understand. He knows those who never will.

'My Father loves me and He knows how much I love my sheep. Enough to die for them – and then to be given my life back again.'

Jesus pauses.

Then, 'This is what I *choose*,' He finishes. 'And this is what God has commanded me to do.'

There are whispers among the onlookers; chunters among the Pharisees.

'This Man's mad! He must be mad to talk like this. Why are we listening to Him?'

But not all of them feel the same.

'If this Man is mad,' they say, 'then how *can* He talk like this? And how can a madman make blind people able to see?'

Paul feels a lump rise in his throat. He doesn't want it to be there. He tries to swallow it away but it sits where it is and his eyes smart with tears.

*Jesus, the good shepherd.* He turns the words over inside his head.

*Jesus, the good shepherd. Ready to die for His sheep.*

# CHAPTER 11
## Wood
### (John 11:1–7,11–15)

Isaac stands at a workbench and bangs his hammer down to knock in a last nail.

Topz' friend from Capernaum, the fishing village, flips over the small stool he's made, to inspect it. He places it, legs down, on the ground and presses on it with one hand to test it.

'Finished,' he announces. 'Who wants to give it a try?'

Sarah looks uncertain.

'It's fine,' Isaac says. 'Stools are for sitting on. It's designed to hold your weight.'

'Erm … What if it doesn't?' Sarah asks.

'It will,' insists Isaac.

'Anyway,' chuckles John, 'if it doesn't, it's hardly a long way to fall, is it?'

'It's not *that*,' Sarah frowns. She tosses her hair back impatiently. 'I just don't want to be the one to break it.'

Isaac reaches out. He picks Saucy carefully from Sarah's arms. Saucy stares at him through puzzled eyes as she feels his hands around her middle, her legs left dangling in midair.

She looks even more surprised when Isaac plonks her down on his newly made stool. Surprised and a little resentful. Sarah's arms create a warm and comfy cradle for her. The seat of the wooden stool is hard and cold. One of her back paws slips off the edge. She lifts it up, and instantly the other slides down. She snatches that one up quickly, too, glances at Sarah to judge the distance, and makes the leap back up towards her.

Sarah catches her. Her eyes flick towards Isaac. They both laugh.

'Sorry Saucy doesn't like your stool,' she splutters.

Isaac shrugs his shoulders. 'I'll have to work on something just for cats.'

'Can *I* sit on your stool?' asks Paul.

'Go ahead,' replies Isaac.

Paul lowers himself onto it. He wriggles a little, testing how sturdy it is.

'This is so cool,' he grins. 'I wish I could make a stool.'

'Well … I could teach you. I could teach you the things my uncle's teaching me.'

Isaac's uncle is a carpenter. The boy is staying with him for a few weeks so that he can learn about handling wood. About designing and building. He already knows quite a lot – he's been teaching himself woodwork back at home in Capernaum – but he wants to be able to make bigger things. Better things. Things that are useful, like stools and chairs, chests and tables. Perhaps even animal shelters.

Things that one day he might be able to make and sell.

Josie's eyes light up. 'Oh, teach me, too!' she beams.

From the far end of the street, Benny's voice rings out.

'Josie! Paul! All of you!'

Benny pelts towards them.

He reaches them and, 'Jesus is going to Bethany,' he puffs, gulping as he gasps for breath. 'He's leaving right now.'

Paul looks up at him from his perch on the stool. 'I thought He was staying round here for a few more days.'

Benny shakes his head. 'It's His friend. Lazarus.'

Two days before, Lazarus' sisters, Mary and Martha, had sent Jesus a message to tell Him their brother was ill. But Jesus hadn't gone to see him.

He'd said, 'This illness won't end with Lazarus' death. This has happened so that people will see God's glory. And there will be glory for God's Son, too.'

'Is Lazarus still ill?' asks Josie. 'Has he got worse?'

Under Benny's fringe, a film of sweat glistens. He pushes back his hair and wipes it away with the back of one hand. 'Jesus just said that His friend had fallen asleep and He was going to wake him up.'

'If he's asleep, that's a good thing,' says Isaac. 'Sleep helps you get better.'

Benny glances at him. 'That's exactly what the disciples said. But Jesus didn't mean he's gone to sleep. Jesus told His disciples that Lazarus has died. And He said He was glad He wasn't with him when it happened.'

'No!' cries Sarah. 'No, Jesus would never say anything like that.'

'He did though! And He said that this is what would make the disciples believe in Him.'

Isaac and the Gang don't move. They stare at Benny, confused. They can't understand what he's talking about.

Benny sighs. 'Listen. I can't explain it any better than I have. All I know is that Lazarus is dead in Bethany and Jesus is on His way to see Him. So we can either sit here and try to figure out what on earth that means, or –'

'Or we can get after Him,' says John. 'Because if we miss this – I think **WE MIGHT MISS SOMETHING REALLY BIG**.'

# CHAPTER 12
## The Life
### (John 11:17–44)

Bethany, where Lazarus lives with his sisters, Martha and Mary, is still not quite in sight when Jesus hears the news.

Lazarus is dead, yes, but he's already been buried, too. Four days ago.

'Look,' says Josie. She points to a woman who makes her way slowly towards Jesus. The woman holds her head down and her shoulders droop. 'Isn't that Martha? We've seen her before, d'you remember? She was the one who was cross with her sister for sitting down and listening to Jesus while she was left doing all the work.'

Martha looks sad and worn. Her eyes are dull. They seem sunk into deep, dark circles in her face. She hasn't slept – not properly – in days.

And she has lost her brother.

Lots of people have arrived at her house to comfort her and Mary. Lots of people have been very kind.

But the two women have lost the brother they love.

And they're heartbroken.

'Oh, my Lord.' Martha's voice is hopeless. She can barely speak. Her eyes feel so sore and heavy from crying, she is hardly able to lift them to Jesus at all.

'My Lord, if only You had been there. Then my brother wouldn't have died. He'd still be with us right now.'

She pauses as a sob catches in her throat. 'But in spite of that, Lord, I do know that whatever You ask God for – even now – He will give it to You.'

Jesus stares down at her. She hurts so much. The pain of losing her brother aches through every part of her.

He says, 'Your brother will come back to life, Martha.'

Martha nods. 'I know,' she sobs. 'I know that God will call Lazarus to live with Him forever.'

'Listen to me,' Jesus says. 'I am the resurrection. I am the life. Everyone who believes in me will live forever, even though they have to die. But for all those people who live and believe in me – death won't be the end! Do you believe this, Martha?'

Martha screws up her eyes. She searches Jesus' face through the mist of tears.

'I do, Lord. I do believe that You are God's Son who has come to live on earth. You are the Messiah.'

Josie stares. 'If Jesus says He's the resurrection,' she whispers, 'that means He must have power over death.'

'He does,' says Sarah. 'We know He does.'

A shadow of doubt crosses Benny's face. 'But Lazarus died a while ago. He's been dead for four days.'

Paul gazes over towards Jesus. 'And what about His own death?'

Topz turn to look at him.

'Jesus is going to die,' Paul mutters. 'That's what He keeps saying. Will He have power over His own death, too?'

Jesus asks Martha to go home and send her sister, Mary, to see Him.

When Mary appears a short while later, the house guests and the well-wishers have followed her.

'That's that Man, Jesus, isn't it?' one or two of them say. 'We thought Mary was going to visit her brother's grave.'

Mary hurries to Jesus. Then suddenly, she is on her knees in front of Him. Her face crumples as tears stream down her cheeks.

'Oh, Lord, I wish You'd been here!' Just like Martha, she cries, 'If You'd only been here, my brother wouldn't have died!'

The people with Mary cry, too.

And Jesus feels every last, hopeless teardrop.

'Where is Lazarus buried?' He asks at last.

'Come with us, we'll show You,' someone answers.

Josie gasps. 'Look at Him! Oh, just look at Him!'

There are tears in Jesus' eyes, too. As He blinks, they spill onto His face. He doesn't wipe them away.

It's not just Josie who notices. Other people see Jesus' sadness.

'He must have loved Lazarus very much,' one of them says.

But there are others again who seem almost cross with Him. 'Isn't this the Man who made a blind person able to see again?' they grumble.

'So why couldn't He have saved Lazarus' life?'

If Jesus hears them, He says nothing. He and His disciples follow the troop of mourners to Lazarus' grave. Martha has joined them again, too.

Topz trail along a little way behind. They don't want to be in the way – don't want Mary and Martha to think they're poking their noses in where they don't belong.

At a cave with a stone pushed up across the opening, the people stop.

'This is where we buried him,' someone says.

Jesus' disciples stand close around Him, but He hardly seems to notice them. He hardly seems to notice anyone. All His attention is fixed on the grave in front of Him.

'Take away the stone,' He says. 'Now.'

Martha looks horrified. 'But … Well, no, Lord. Lazarus has been dead for four days! If we open the grave now, the … the smell, Lord … it'll be terrible.'

'Martha, Martha!' says Jesus. 'What have I told you? If you believe – just believe! – then you will see God's glory!'

Martha sucks in a breath. She glances towards the friends and family who stand with her. She gives them the tiniest of nods. And together, a group of them heave the stone out of the way.

Topz stand and stare. Silent.

Jesus looks up. He prays. 'Father, thank You for listening to me. I know You always listen. But I say this now so that everyone here will believe that You have sent me.'

He lowers His gaze. 'Lazarus!'

His voice is loud. Powerful. **'LAZARUS! COME OUT!'**

No one moves. Topz can't breathe. They're so stunned, they don't even *notice* they've stopped breathing!

And suddenly, in the entrance of the cave, a figure stands.

There are gasps from the onlookers; open mouths, wide eyes.

The figure is wrapped up in cloth: his grave clothes. His face is covered, too.

Paul gulps. He squints hard into the shadows, blinks at the shape through his glasses. He finds his voice.

'Is it him? Is it really Lazarus?'

'Undo the cloths.' This time, Jesus speaks quietly. Calmly. 'It's all right,' He says. 'He's all right now.'

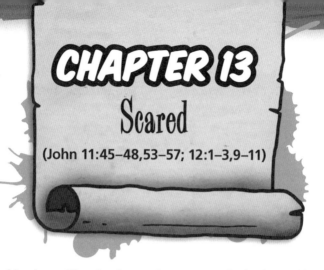

# CHAPTER 13
## Scared
(John 11:45–48,53–57; 12:1–3,9–11)

Paul is alone. The day is nearly over. He sits by himself on a hillside, looking across the plains towards Jerusalem. The city streets and buildings spread towards the horizon. People bustle about their lives there, but he's too far away to see them.

And tomorrow – Jesus will arrive.

Paul hugs his knees into his chest. He doesn't like this feeling. He hates it. The feeling that something terrible is going to happen. That he doesn't understand what or how. All he knows is that he and the rest of the Gang are helpless to do anything to stop it.

And even if they could – he knows that God doesn't want them to.

*I'm scared, God.*

Paul speaks the words out into the empty space all around him. Will God hear them?

He needs God to hear them.

*One by one. The days are ticking by. And with each day and each miracle Jesus makes happen, the terrible thing gets closer. I don't even know what it is.*

*But I have this feeling inside me and when Jesus talks about the future – about leaving – my stomach twists into a knot. And it gets tighter and tighter.*

*I want to understand, God. I want to make sense of what Jesus is saying, but I can't.*

*Perhaps I never will.*

*At least, not until after …*

*Jesus brought Lazarus back to life. He asked You to do it for Him, didn't He, and You did. And just like Jesus said they would, lots more people believed in Him after that. Because they could see Your glory. And they could see Your glory reflected in Jesus because everything He does is what You've told Him to do. It's why You sent Him. When people saw Lazarus step out of the cave, what else could they do? They had to believe!*

*Except that some people – I don't know if they thought it was a trick, or what – but they went to the Pharisees and told them about it. And then the Pharisees got in a proper panic. They said that if Jesus was allowed to carry on with His miracles, then everyone would end up believing in Him and they'd lose all their power. People would follow Jesus and His teaching rather than the Pharisees and their Law. And then the Pharisees wouldn't be the ones in charge anymore.*

*So now, they're plotting something. Against Jesus. Something bad. Instead of hearing about His miracles and realising that only Someone sent by God could do any of those things – instead of believing in Him and that He's telling the truth –* **THEY'RE MAKING A PLAN TO KILL HIM.**

Jesus hid out for a bit. Somewhere near the desert.
He said it's not His time yet, but not time for what?

Lots of people are going to Jerusalem just now.
It's nearly time for the Passover Festival, when Jewish
people remember how You saved them all. Another
time, a long time ago, when You saved all their lives.
And people are asking, 'Will Jesus be at the Festival?
He won't turn up, will He? Surely He won't!' Because
the chief priests and the Pharisees have put out orders
that if anyone sees Him or knows where He is, they've
got to tell them. So they can arrest Him.

Jesus went back to Bethany a few days ago. He had
dinner with Martha and Mary.

And Lazarus.

The man He brought back to life.

As soon as people heard Jesus was there, they were
off like a shot to Bethany. They wanted to see Him, and
they wanted to see Lazarus. See the man who was dead
but is now alive, with their own eyes.

Only, now the Pharisees and the chief priests want
to kill Lazarus, too. Lazarus is walking, living, breathing
proof of who Jesus is and of what He can do. So they
want to get rid of him. Before even more people believe
in Jesus and stop following their Law ...

Tomorrow, Jesus goes to Jerusalem. To celebrate the
Passover there, along with all the other Jews.

And the terrible thing will be one day closer.

I'm scared, God ...

'you will not always have me.' (John 12:8)

# CHAPTER 14

## In Charge

### (John 12:12–19)

The air throbs with excitement.

There are people everywhere. They line the roadside all the way into Jerusalem. They've come for the Passover Festival. They've also heard about Lazarus. The news of his new miracle life has spread quickly, like a raging fire.

'Jesus? Who is this amazing Jesus?' they want to know.

So the moment they hear that Jesus is on His way to Jerusalem, they're running out to meet Him. They're laughing and stumbling into each other, and laughing again. They bring branches from palm trees to wave and to lay on the road Jesus will pass along.

And they cheer and shout at the tops of their voices: 'Praise God! Praise Him and may He bless the One who's coming – the One who comes in His name! The King of Israel!'

The Pharisees can't do a thing to stop them. Not yet. They can only grit their teeth and mutter to each other, 'Nothing we do makes any difference. Look at all these people! Is everyone in the whole world following Jesus now?'

Topz push their way through the growing crowd with Isaac until they find a space at the side of the road. Benny trips on a palm branch. He doesn't know if it's been dropped or laid down with the others, but he picks it up anyway so that he has something to wave.

'I want Jesus to look at me,' he grins. 'I just want Him to see me as He goes past.'

Paul stands behind him. He's quiet.

'Are you all right?' asks Sarah. 'Can you see?'

Paul nods. He can't really see over Benny's head, but it doesn't matter. He wants to hide. He doesn't want to be noticed. All around him, people are happy. The shouting and cheering grows louder. Eyes sparkle; hands clap.

But inside him, his heart just wants to cry.

John steps back into the space next to him. Gruff is tucked under his arm. The dog doesn't seem too happy about it but there are so many people and John doesn't want him to get trampled. Besides, he wants to be on the lookout for Jesus, not for Gruff.

'I know what you're thinking,' John says. 'How can anything bad be about to happen? These people love Jesus. They'd never turn against Him.'

Paul doesn't answer. He can't. There are tears threatening at the backs of his eyes again, so he keeps his head down.

'Whatever happens, God's in charge,' John says. 'Jesus knows it. And He's coming back, Paul. Jesus only ever tells the truth. He says He's coming back, so He'll be back.'

Suddenly, the crowd noise explodes. If John had said anything else, Paul wouldn't have been able to hear it.

Just there, at the very far end of the road where it unravels this side of the horizon, is Jesus. **HE RIDES ON A DONKEY.**

John nudges Paul and points, until slowly Paul lifts his eyes to see the Man everyone's cheering for as He arrives in Jerusalem.

Paul has to stand on tiptoe to make Him out properly. And when he catches sight of Him – he stares. Not at Jesus. He's seen Him so many times before.

It's the donkey he can't take his eyes from.

It's the donkey that all of a sudden stops the crying in his heart and lifts the dark cloud over his head. Words he's read before spring into his mind. Words of Scripture.

He leans towards John. He puts his mouth to John's ear and shouts to make sure John hears him.

'I've read this! I've read that Jesus will arrive in Jerusalem like this! Riding on a donkey. I've read it – and it was written about before Jesus was even born!'

*'Shout for joy, you people of Jerusalem! Look, your king is coming to you! He comes triumphant and victorious, but humble and riding on a donkey'* (Zechariah 9:9).

John turns to look at him. He smiles.

And Paul understands – properly understands at last – that whatever happens now, **GOD IS IN CHARGE.**

# CHAPTER 15
## How to be Humble
(John 13:1–21)

'I should have brought my tools with me.' Isaac stands, hands on hips, looking down at a heap of scrap wood piled at the edge of a street on the outskirts of Jerusalem. 'We could have made something with this.'

'There must be enough here to build a tree house,' says Josie.

Paul glances round. 'Not much in the way of trees though.'

'Not here, maybe,' says Dave. 'But we should take some of it with us when we go back to your uncle, Isaac. Even if we can't make a tree house, you could teach us how to make something.'

Isaac uses his foot to turn over some of the old planks. There are nails sticking out of a few of them, so he's careful.

'I wonder if Jesus still makes things,' he says. 'Do you think He still thinks about His life when He was a carpenter?'

'Probably,' answers Josie. 'Whoever you are, you always remember where you came from, don't you? The things you've done.'

'Unless you have really bad memory,' says Paul.

Isaac kicks over another piece of splintered wood. 'I'd like Jesus to know I want to be a carpenter,' he says.

'I'm sure He will,' smiles Josie. 'I'm sure He does.'

It's the day before the Passover Festival. Jerusalem tingles with excitement as people gather together and get ready for the celebration.

Jesus' disciples prepare, too. As Topz and Isaac head further into the city, they see them carrying food into a house down a narrow street.

'That must be where they're staying,' says Danny. 'D'you think Jesus is there now?'

Sarah smiles. 'Yes.' She points towards a narrow window. 'There He is.'

Jesus stands in front of it. They can hear His disciples talking to each other. Talking to Him. Through the doorway, they can see them setting the table for supper. It's a long table. It needs to be to allow all thirteen men to sit around it.

While they are eating, Jesus pushes back His chair and stands up. He rolls up His sleeves, fetches a towel and ties it round His waist.

Then He fills a basin with some water and, starting at one end of the table, He crouches down to wash the feet of the man who sits there.

'What's He doing?' asks Danny. The room is quite dark. It's hard to see.

'I think …' John murmurs, 'I think Jesus is washing that disciple's feet.'

Sarah shakes her head. 'He can't be. He's God's Son. Why would He do that? And His friends know who He is – why would they *let* Him do that?'

'Ssh.' John puts a finger to his lips. 'Listen.'

The disciples seem as stunned as Topz. They don't say a word. They just stare at Jesus as He squats in front of them, one after the other, washes their feet and dries them again with the towel He has tied around His waist.

There is silence. Until it's Jesus' friend Peter's turn.

'You're not going to wash my feet, too, Lord – are You?' He gazes at Jesus. He frowns at Him. Why would He do a job so dirty? So … humble?

'You don't understand now,' Jesus answers. 'I know that. But later on, you will.'

Peter throws up his hands. He looks around at the other disciples who still sit at the table. He shakes his head firmly.

'No, no never,' he says. 'You will never wash my feet, Lord!'

Jesus doesn't stand up. He doesn't take His eyes from Peter's eyes.

'Peter, if you don't allow me to wash your feet, then you will not be my disciple anymore.'

Peter's frown deepens. He opens his mouth quickly to answer – perhaps to argue – but he is so shocked that no words come out.

Until, into the quiet he blurts, 'Then, Lord, please don't just wash my feet. Wash my hands and wash my head, too!'

Jesus gives him a half smile. 'When someone has a bath,' He says, 'they come out completely clean. It's just their feet that will need another wash. All of you, my friends – you are all clean.'

Sarah blinks through the darkness. 'God makes us clean,' she murmurs. 'When we believe in Jesus, God give us brand-new, clean lives. All the things we do wrong are washed away. Like we wash dirt away in a bath.

'But we still have to go back to Him. We try but we still get things wrong. So then we need to go back to God to say sorry again. So that He can *keep* us clean.'

Jesus glances round at His friends. 'You are all clean,' He says again. 'All except one of you.'

The disciples exchange looks. What does Jesus mean?

They say nothing. They sit and wait. Until He has washed the feet of each of them. Until He has undone the towel at His waist, rolled down His sleeves, and sat at the table again.

'Do you understand what I have just done?' He asks. 'Do you know why I've done it?'

The disciples stare at Jesus with blank faces. They *want* to understand. But they feel as though they know nothing.

'You call me "Lord" and "Teacher",' Jesus says. 'That's the right thing to do. That's what I am. So I, who am your Lord and your Teacher – I have washed your feet. And I've done it to show you how I want you to care for each other,' He explains.

Still the disciples gaze at Him. What is it He wants them to learn?

Just outside the door, Topz are unsure, too.

'I want you to do for each other,' Jesus says, 'exactly what I've just done for you. I want you to serve each other. And if you do,' He adds, 'you will be much happier for it.'

The puzzled expression doesn't clear from Isaac's face. 'Why will we be happier?'

'I think,' says Danny, 'Jesus means that if we do as He says and follow His example, then God can bless us. We'll be happier if we obey Him. Jesus has shown His disciples that being their Teacher – being their Lord – doesn't matter. How *important* we are doesn't matter.

'What matters is being humble. Being prepared to help each other out in any way we can. In any way that's needed. Never feeling that we're too special or somehow above doing something.'

'Jesus is above everything,' Paul nods. 'He's Lord of the whole world. The whole universe! But He just got down on the floor and washed His disciples' feet.'

He pushes his glasses up his nose. He looks at Isaac and into the faces of his friends.

### *'THAT'S THE MOST HUMBLE THING I'VE EVER SEEN.'*

'There's something else,' Jesus says. 'I have chosen you and I know you. But a long time ago, something was written about me. A verse of Scripture. A prophecy, and it has to come true.'

Jesus pauses. The words seem difficult for Him to say. As if it hurts Him to speak them.

'The verse says that the man who has shared food with me ... will turn against me. I want you to know this before it happens – and then when it does happen, you will completely believe that I am who I say I am.

'Here's the truth again,' Jesus adds. 'Whoever welcomes who I send to them, welcomes me, too. Whoever welcomes me – well – they welcome the One who sent me.'

He sighs. A sigh that's deep. That aches with pain. He looks up and His eyes are full of shadows.

'One more truth, then,' He says. 'One of you will point the finger at me. One of you will give me away to the people who hate me.'

# CHAPTER 16
## God on the Earth
### (John 13:22–14:14)

Saucy stirs in Sarah's arms but Sarah clings on to her tightly. It's dark now. Late.

'No, Saucy, keep still.' Her voice is no more than a whisper. She doesn't want to be heard or seen. She doesn't want any of them to be spotted near the doorway to the house. Listening, watching. To be told to go away would be unbearable.

The moments are ticking by. The moments of Jesus' life on earth.

And Sarah can't stand the thought of having to leave Him now.

Inside the house, the disciples look confused and unhappy.

Peter gets the attention of the man sitting next to Jesus. 'Who's Jesus talking about?' he hisses to him. 'Ask Him.'

The man gives a little nod of his head. He leans towards Jesus. He asks Him in a low voice that Topz can only just hear, 'Who are You talking about, Lord? Who is going to give You away?'

Jesus doesn't answer at once.

'I will take a piece of bread and dip it into the sauce from our meal,' He says finally. 'I will give it to one of you … It's him.'

Jesus does what He says. He picks up some bread, dips it. Then He turns. He holds it out towards the disciple called Judas.

And Judas takes it.

Jesus hardly looks at him. He just says, 'Do what you're going to do quickly.'

Judas is the one in their group who takes care of the money. Some of the disciples think perhaps Jesus has asked him to go and buy more food for the Passover meal. Or to give some money to the poor.

But the moment he takes the bread, Judas gets up from the table and heads for the door.

Topz shuffle back quickly into the shadows. Benny pulls Isaac with him.

Judas doesn't seem to notice them as he leaves the house and slinks past. They lose sight of him in the darkness. They listen until his footfalls die away.

Until there is silence.

'We should go after him,' mutters Benny. 'We should try to stop him. We know he's going to betray Jesus – Jesus says so. Are we just going to stand here and let him?'

John shakes his head. He looks down at Gruff, who paws at his leg. He crouches to pick him up. Then he stands, eyes fixed on his dog, not on Benny.

'We're not going to do anything, Benny,' he murmurs. 'We can't.'

Benny's forehead scrunches into a deep frown. 'Why not?'

John shrugs. 'Because it's not up to us.'

Inside the house, no one speaks. The disciples are still puzzled. Now they're uneasy, too.

'It's time for the Son of Man's glory to be discovered,' Jesus says. 'And it's time for God's glory to be discovered through Him.'

The faintest of smiles crosses His face. But it's not a happy smile. It's heavy with sadness.

'I'm not going to be with you for much longer,' He begins again. 'You will look for me, but you can't go where I'm going.

'I have a new commandment for you, though. **YOU MUST LOVE EACH OTHER.** In just the way that I have loved you, you must love each other. You see, if you show that you love each other, then other people will see – other people will know – that you are my disciples.'

Peter can't keep quiet any longer. 'But where are You going, Lord? *Where?*'

Jesus' eyes flick towards him. 'It's not somewhere you can follow me,' He answers. 'Not now. But you will follow me later. Another time.'

Peter springs to his feet. 'Why can't I follow You now? Just tell me! Because, Lord, I am ready to die for You!'

Jesus still stares at him. He gazes into him, right inside him.

'Are you, Peter? Are you sure you're ready to die for me?'

Jesus shakes His head. Once again, the smile lifts His mouth but there's no light in His eyes.

'The truth is,' He says, 'before you hear the cock crow, you will say three times that you don't even know me.'

Peter looks stunned. Topz, too.

'But Peter loves Jesus!' gasps Josie. 'He'd do anything for Him.'

Jesus doesn't wait for Peter to reply. He looks back at His other friends, still gathered round the table.

'You mustn't be worried or upset,' He says. 'Just keep believing in God. And believe in me, too. My Father's house has many rooms, and I will go there and I will get a place ready for you. I wouldn't say this if I wasn't going to do it.

'And then, I'll come back,' He goes on. 'I'll come back and I'll take you there with me, so that we can be together again. You know the way that will take you to where I'm going.'

Thomas, another disciple, interrupts. 'But we don't

know *where* You're going, Lord. If we don't know *where* You're going, how can we know the way there?'

'Because I am the way,' Jesus says. 'I am the way and the truth and the life. The only way to reach the Father is through me. Because you know me, you know my Father, too. You do know Him. You see Him in me.'

Philip, who's also at the table, wants so much to understand, too. He wants to follow Jesus' instructions. To make sure that one day he will be with Jesus again.

'Jesus,' he begs, 'oh, Jesus, please show us the Father, then. All we want is to see Him.'

Jesus sighs. He shakes His head. 'Oh, Philip, how long have I been with you now? And still you don't know me? I say it again, if you have seen me, then you have seen my Father, too. Is it so hard for you to believe that I am a part of my Father?' He asks. 'And that my Father is a part of me?'

He looks round at the other men. 'Everything I'm saying to you – it doesn't come from me,' He continues. 'This is my Father's work, my Father who will always be a part of me. You must believe me when I tell you that we are a part of each other. And if you won't believe my words, at least believe me because of the things you have seen me do!

'And honestly, people who believe in me will be able to do what I have done. In fact, they'll be able to do even bigger things, because I am going back to my Father, and I will do whatever you ask in my name. That way, the Father's glory will go on being shown through me.

'So talk to me – *pray* to me – and if it's what God wants for you or for someone else, it will happen. I will do it for you.'

Paul shivers. It's cold now. He feels chilled in the darkness.

'I've got this auntie,' he says slowly, 'who says I look just like my dad. "Two peas in a pod" she calls us. It's annoying sometimes because I'm still growing. And when I'm properly grown up, I might not look like my dad at all. Because I'm me, Paul, and I'm not like anyone else in the whole world. Not completely.

'But even if I don't look anything like my dad, or my mum, when I grow up – I'll still always be a part of them. And they'll always be a part of me. We belong to each other …'

His voice trails off. He hugs his arms around himself; tries to keep warm. 'And Jesus will always belong to God, won't He? Because God's His Father. You can't believe in One without believing in the Other.

'Jesus is here because of His Father. It's His Father who sent Him. And His Father's inside Him.'

Paul looks up towards the sky. The deep-black sky, so heavy with clouds. He shudders again. Not with cold this time, but with the huge, enormous miracle of it all.

'This is the most amazing time ever for the whole world. Right now.

'Jesus is God brought down to the earth … And we're looking at Him.'

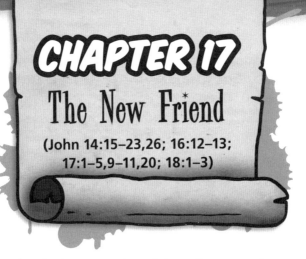

# CHAPTER 17
## The New Friend
### (John 14:15–23,26; 16:12–13; 17:1–5,9–11,20; 18:1–3)

Lost in the shadows near Jesus' door, Dave crouches down. He leans his back against the stone wall of the building. He crosses his arms and tucks his hands into them to keep them warm.

'We should have brought some food,' he whispers.

Danny shrugs. 'We didn't know we'd be here so long.'

'It's usually Benny who's after food,' grunts Paul.

'Don't really care tonight,' Benny mutters in reply. 'I am freezing, though.'

The moon must be somewhere overhead, but they don't know where. They can't see it. A thick blanket of cloud blots it out – stops even a pin-prick of starlight peeking through.

Still inside the house, Jesus says to His disciples, 'If you love me, then try to do everything I have told you to do. And I will ask my Father to send Someone else to be with you,' He says. 'Another Friend. A Helper. I'm talking about God's Holy Spirit. When He comes to you, He will stay with you forever. He will show you who God really is!

'And when I leave, you won't be on your own anyway. Not for long. Because I will come back. I will live again! And when I live again, you will live, too. You will *know* – for absolute certain – that I belong to my Father. That you belong to me. And that I belong to you.

'You see,' says Jesus, 'if anyone hears my teaching and does what I ask them to do, that shows that they love me. And my Father will love them for loving me!

'I will love them, too. And I'll make sure that they know who I am.'

Josie hunches down next to Dave. Isaac and the rest of the Gang huddle together. Sarah buries her hands in Saucy's fur for warmth; John cuddles Gruff more tightly. He can feel the pulsing of the little dog's heartbeat.

'It's true,' Josie murmurs. 'If we obey Jesus and we love Him, then He does show us who He is. He's there always. Right beside us. And the more we spend time with Him and the more we talk to Him and trust Him, the more we can feel that He's there. The more we can *know* that He's there.'

*'Whoever loves me will obey my teaching … and my Father and I will come to him and live with him.'*
*(John 14:23)*

'Don't forget your new Friend!' Jesus says. 'God will send Him to you – His Holy Spirit. His Spirit will teach you everything! And He'll make sure you remember everything I've already taught you.'

Jesus pauses a moment. He takes in a long breath. His heart is still full of the things He wants to tell.

'Remember this: when the Spirit, your Friend, comes to you, He will show you the truth of everything I am saying. He will help you understand all of this. All that's about to happen. And He won't say anything that doesn't come from God. He won't speak a word that doesn't come from *me*. Because everything God, my Father, has is mine. And every word that comes out of my mouth comes from my Father – and these are the words I will give the Spirit to speak to you.'

Dave leans forward. He screws up his eyes against the dark to try to see inside the house. He makes out the dim figure of Jesus, who looks up towards heaven. Towards His Father.

He watches Jesus as He prays:

'Father … It's time. Please honour me, so that I may honour You. You gave me the power to lead people to a life that will last forever. And that everlasting life means knowing You, the one and only real God, and knowing me, the One You have sent.

'I have done as You asked me to, Father. I have uncovered You to the world! And now my work is finished. Please let me be beside You again now – alive and shining with the glory I had with You long before You had even made this world.

'I pray for the people You have given to me. I am coming back to You, Father, but they will still be here. Keep them safe. Help them to live as one body of people – strong and believing and full of hope so that they can encourage each other.

'And I pray for all the *others*, too, Father. All of those who will believe in me one day, because of the message that these first believers will spread.

'I pray that they will be one body of people, too. One body that loves You and loves me, so that the rest of the world will start to believe!

'You have given me all these people, Father. And one day, I want them to be with me. With You.

'Always.'

Sarah's crying. John feels her sobs where her shoulder touches his.

'What is it?' he asks. 'What's wrong?'

For a moment, she can't speak. Then, 'You heard it, didn't you?' she gulps. 'You heard what Jesus said. We're the "others", John. **WE JUST LISTENED TO JESUS PRAY FOR US.**'

There's a scraping of benches on the floor. Jesus and His disciples get up from the table at last, ready to leave the house.

Topz slip back, further out of sight.

'Where will they go?' asks Isaac.

'Dunno.' Benny shrugs. 'But where they go – we go.'

They wait.

They see Jesus and His bewildered friends step out into the coldness of the night and walk quietly away.

And they follow them.

There's a brook called Kidron. Jesus and the disciples cross over it. They don't just wander. They seem to know exactly where they're going.

Topz cross the water, too. They see the group ahead of them walk into a garden. They steal through after them and hide just inside the gate. It's good that the clouds block out the moon tonight. It makes the shadows deeper. Blacker.

So much easier not to be seen.

Topz have hardly had time to position themselves out of sight, when they hear the sound of marching on the road outside the garden.

More men step in through the gate. They carry weapons and lanterns. They look like soldiers and guards. That's the way they're dressed.

But the man at the front – the man who seems to be leading them – he's not a soldier. As he turns to throw a quick glance over his shoulder, Topz just manage to catch a glimpse of his face. His eyes are dimly lit in the flicker of lantern light.

'No!' Josie breathes. But she knows exactly who it is. They all do.

The man who leads the soldiers against Jesus is the man who left the house first that evening. The man who took the bread Jesus offered him.

Judas.

The man who would betray Him.

# CHAPTER 18
## The Price to Pay
**(John 18:4–12)**

Topz shrink back into the gloom. As far as they can.
Sarah and John still hold on tightly to Saucy and Gruff.
John strokes Gruff's ears to keep him quiet. Gruff
always likes that.

Jesus doesn't try to hide. He knows full well why the
soldiers have come. He knows that Judas has led them
to the garden. It's a place He and the disciples have
met in before.

Jesus steps into the lantern light. 'Who are you
looking for?' He asks.

One of them answers with a snarl: 'Jesus of Nazareth.'

*'Why?'* Paul hisses. 'Why are there soldiers here
for Jesus? With weapons! Who do they think He is?
What on earth do they think He's going to do?'

Josie nudges him. She puts a finger to her lips.
He needs to be quiet.

Jesus doesn't hesitate. 'I am the Man you're looking
for,' He says.

Judas doesn't take his eyes off Him. But the moment
Jesus says who He is, the soldiers stumble backwards.

They're shocked. Bewildered. This Man doesn't try to run away. He stands His ground and stares right at them.

He gives Himself up to them.

Jesus asks them again: 'Who is it you want?'

Again, 'Jesus of Nazareth!' they announce.

'And I have told you already that I am Jesus of Nazareth,' Jesus replies. 'So if it's me you want, there's no point keeping these others hanging around.' He lifts a hand to indicate His disciples. 'Let them go.'

There's a sudden movement. Peter shoves his friends out of the way.

With a flash of brightness, he draws a sword, the blade caught for a second in the light from the lanterns. Then he swipes it down and strikes at one of the men who have come for Jesus. A servant who works for the high priest at the Temple in Jerusalem.

Josie's hands fly to her mouth. Topz look on, horrified.

'That's enough, Peter!' cries Jesus. 'Put your sword away. Now! Whatever my Father wants me to go through – whatever it is I have to suffer – *I will do it*.'

'But why?' Josie sobs. 'Why does God want Jesus to suffer?'

This is horrible. Dreadful. That feeling – that aching, miserable, awful feeling – the one all of Topz have had for so long – this is why. It's happening right in front of their eyes.

While Judas watches, the soldiers arrest Jesus. They grab hold of Him. He doesn't try to run away. He doesn't make any trouble at all. But they still tie Him up. They still treat Him like a criminal.

Then they haul Him away.

The disciples stand helplessly and watch. Their Friend. Their Teacher. Their *Lord!* How can this be happening to Him?

Then Peter and one of the others follow after Him.

'We should go, too,' mutters Paul. 'We need to see where they're taking Him.'

Topz slip out from their hiding place.

'He'll be all right,' murmurs Isaac. 'He will. God won't let anything bad happen to His Son. He won't. He couldn't!'

Sarah slides Saucy into the bag over her shoulder. She reaches out a hand. She puts it on Isaac's arm. He turns. Stops walking a moment.

'God loves Jesus,' Sarah whispers. Her eyes glisten with tears. The knot in her throat makes it almost impossible for her to speak. 'But **HE LOVES US**, too,' she manages. 'And it's because He loves us so much that all of this has to happen.'

'All of what?' Isaac snaps.

His voice and his face are usually kind and gentle. Not now.

Harshly he repeats, *'All of what?'*

'It's a punishment ...' Sarah thinks she'll choke on her sobs. 'It's *our* punishment, Isaac. The punishment of everyone in the whole world. Because we do things wrong! We do things that God tells us not to do. Things that are bad for us, things that make Him sad! And those wrong things have to be paid for. They have to be punished. Only ...'

She stops again. She swallows hard. She has to get the words out.

'Only, you see, Isaac, God isn't going to punish us. He's going to forgive us!

'But before He can forgive us, someone has to pay for the wrong things that we do. That's the only way for us to be friends with God again – if someone pays. If someone gives up their life.

'And that someone is Jesus ...'

Isaac stares at her in disbelief. His eyes glitter furiously. As if it's her fault. As if she should be able to stop it.

'But Jesus hasn't done anything wrong!' he snarls.

'No.' Sarah shakes her head miserably. 'No, He hasn't. But this is why He's here, Isaac. This is what He came to do. And He knows everything that's going to happen to Him.'

'Sarah!' Up ahead of them Dave calls. 'Sarah, come on, we're losing them!'

Sarah gazes back at Isaac a moment more. Then she brushes the tears from her face and hurries on.

# CHAPTER 19
## He's Always Known
### (John 18:17–27)

'Who lives here?'

Paul peers into the courtyard of a large house. The house Jesus has just been marched into.

There's a girl at the gate. 'Annas,' she says. 'He's one of the chief priests. I work for him. You've heard of Caiaphas?'

'I think so,' nods Paul.

'Well, I should hope you have! He's the high priest at the Temple. Anyway, Annas is his father-in-law,' the girl says.

Paul can see Peter in the courtyard.

The girl spots him, too. She walks over to him. 'I know you, don't I?' she asks. 'I've seen you. With Him. With that Jesus. You're one of His friends.'

Paul watches as Peter lowers his head and shakes it. 'Not me,' he grunts. 'I'm not one of them.'

Paul frowns.

Danny catches sight of his face. 'What is it?' he asks.

'Peter,' answers Paul. 'He just told that girl he doesn't

know Jesus. Why would he say that? He's one of Jesus' best friends.'

Danny follows Peter with his eyes as the disciple wanders across the courtyard to hover near some servants and guards. They've built a fire to try to keep themselves warm. Peter is cold, too. He tries to catch some of the heat.

'He's scared,' mutters Danny.

Paul glances at him. 'Why? He's not the one they've arrested.'

'He doesn't know what's going on,' Danny says. 'He doesn't know what they're talking to Jesus about or what's going to happen to Him. And Peter's a friend of His. Whatever happens to Jesus, it could happen to Peter as well because he's a follower,' he adds. 'So d'you know what, Paul? I think if I were him – I'd be scared, too.'

Paul looks back towards the house. 'Well, I don't like this,' he says. 'Any of it. Jesus is in there. I'm going to find out what's going on.'

'Paul! *Paul!*' Danny calls to his friend as loudly as he dares. But it's too late. Paul has already slipped through the gateway and into the courtyard.

*I can do this,* he thinks.

It's better if he's on his own. Without the rest of the Gang. One person's harder to spot than seven. And there's Isaac, too.

As far as he can, Paul keeps to the edge of the yard, near to the wall. There are shadows there – dark places that neither the light from the fire nor the candles burning through the windows of the house can reach.

He sees a man standing with his back to one of the windows. He can hear him talking but he can't make out the words. Is the man speaking to Jesus? Is Jesus somewhere in that room?

Keeping an eye on the group by the fire and making quick scans of the courtyard to check no one else is coming, Paul scoots fast from the wall to the window. He crouches down; makes himself as small as he possibly can. The light that glows from inside the room doesn't pick him up. He might just get away with being here. At least until he knows whether or not he's found Jesus.

And he has.

Paul knows that almost at once.

He can hear the voice better now. He supposes it must belong to Annas, whose house this is.

Annas asks lots of questions. He wants to know about Jesus' followers. About His disciples. He demands to know exactly what Jesus has been saying; what He has been teaching.

Then Paul hears the voice he's been waiting for.

'Why do you ask me all this?' Jesus says. 'I have always taught people in public places. I have spoken to them in synagogues or in the Temple. I have talked to crowds out in the streets. Nowhere have I done anything in secret.

'So why are you asking me these questions? If you want to know what I've been saying, go and speak to the people who have been listening to me. They'll be able to tell you.'

There's the sudden sound of someone being slapped.

Paul flinches. He knows it's Jesus. He can't see but he knows Jesus is being hurt.

'Don't you dare talk to the chief priest like that!' shouts a voice. Not Annas. Probably a guard. Certainly the man who has just hit Jesus.

'Have I said something wrong?' Jesus asks quietly. 'If I have, then tell everyone what it is. But if what I've said is right, then – why have you hit me?'

The voices drop then. There are mutterings and Paul can sense movement in the room. He thinks he hears Annas tell Jesus he's had enough of Him and he's sending Him to the high priest, Caiaphas.

He scuttles back from the window to the safety of the shadows under the wall.

He's about to creep round to the courtyard gate where Topz wait for him, when he hears someone over by the fire ask: 'Hold on a minute – aren't you one of Jesus' friends?'

He turns abruptly. He feels the blood drain from his face. Has he been seen? Is someone talking to him?

No.

The servants and the guards huddled over the warmth of the fire are all looking at Peter.

Peter instantly shakes his head. For the second time that night, he mutters, 'No. No, of course I'm not one of His friends.'

But there's another man by the fire. A relative of the servant Peter had attacked with his sword earlier that night.

'Yes, you are,' says the man. 'I saw you with Him.

I saw you there in the garden.'

'No, you didn't!' snaps Peter. 'Because I wasn't there! I wasn't *with* Jesus in the garden – all right?'

He's hardly finished speaking – he's barely had time to close his frightened mouth – when, somewhere in the distance, **A COCKEREL CROWS.**

Peter hears it. And inside him, he grows ice cold.

Jesus had said it, hadn't He? He'd told Peter that three times Peter would say he didn't know Him. And after the third time, a cock would crow.

Crouching, darting, running, Paul finds a way back to the gate without being spotted. Besides, no one's interested in him. They're interested in Jesus. And in Peter by the fire.

Breathless, Paul stands in the gateway and looks at his friends. His eyes flit from one to the other.

'Where's Isaac?' he asks. The boy is nowhere to be seen.

Sarah's head droops. She shrugs her shoulders. 'Dunno. Haven't seen him since we left the garden.'

Paul glances back towards the house. 'Jesus knows, doesn't He?' he says. 'He really does know everything that's going to happen. He knows how horrible it's going to be. Worse than horrible. Much, much worse. He's always known.

'But He loves God and He loves us.

'So He's going to go through with it anyway.'

# CHAPTER 20

## The Terrible Thing

(John 18:28–30,33–40; 19:1–16)

Topz stay awake all night. Gruff and Saucy doze in fits and starts. They know there's something very wrong. So they stay close.

When Annas has finished with Him, Jesus is taken to see Caiaphas, the high priest. And from Caiaphas, He is led to the palace of Pontius Pilate, who is the Roman governor.

The Roman governor is a powerful man. He can decide what will happen to anyone who is found to be a criminal. A murderer, a thief, anyone. He can have them locked up or set free.

Or he can sentence them to death.

Topz stand outside the palace. A large crowd is gathering around them. They're used to being jostled in crowds who have come to hear Jesus teach; who have come just to catch a glimpse of Him.

But that's not why these people are here. They know that Jesus has been arrested but it's not Him they want to see.

This time, they're here for Pilate.

It's early in the morning. Pilate, the Roman governor, steps outside. He speaks to the chief priests and to the Pharisees.

'Why have you brought this Man to me? What is it He's supposed to have done wrong?'

The priests and the Pharisees shout out, 'He's a criminal! We wouldn't have brought Him to you if we didn't know that He'd been doing and saying bad things!'

Pilate looks puzzled. Worried. He goes back into the palace to talk to Jesus again. He doesn't come out for a long time.

A palace servant pushes through the cluster of people who stand near Topz.

'What's going on?' someone asks him. 'How much longer is this going to take?'

The servant snatches a quick glance behind him, towards the palace. 'I can't say much,' he mutters. 'But Pilate's still asking questions. Lots of questions. He asked this Jesus if He was the King of the Jews. But Jesus didn't say He was or He wasn't. He just asked Pilate if this was something he himself wanted to know, or if it was what other people had told him.

'Then Pilate said, "You've been handed over to me. What is it You've done?"

'But Jesus said something about His kingdom not being on the earth. He said if it was, then His followers would have stopped Him being arrested.

'So Pilate asked Him again: "Are You a king?" But again, Jesus wouldn't say yes or no. He said that He came to earth for one thing and one thing only: to tell the truth.'

Someone shouts, 'There he is!'

The servant jerks around. He sees the governor, Pilate, come out from the palace again.

He tucks his head down and mumbles, 'I've got to go.' And he shuffles off and is quickly lost in the growing crowd.

Pilate stands in front of the waiting people. 'I can't see what wrong this Man is supposed to have done,' he announces. 'There's no reason for me to sentence Him. Now, this is the Passover Festival,' he continues. 'And you have a custom, don't you, that when it's Passover time, I can set free a prisoner for you. So why don't I set this Man, this King of the Jews, free?'

Instantly, the air is filled with shouting and chanting. The crowds don't even stop and think.

'No, we don't want Jesus!' they yell. 'We want you to set Barabbas free! Barabbas!'

'Who?' shouts Paul over the noise. 'Who do they want?'

'Barabbas,' mutters Dave. 'Barabbas is a rebel. They want Pilate to set a rebel free.'

Dave stares round in disbelief at the shouting, flushed, excited faces. The people who punch the air in time to their yells for Barabbas.

He clenches his teeth. 'And they want Jesus, who hasn't done anything wrong,' he hisses, ' to die.'

There's nothing more to say. Nothing Topz can do. Just stand and watch as the terrible thing – the horrible, cruel and terrible thing that they've known is coming – is played out.

Jesus is whipped. Pilate orders it.

And Topz see Him led out afterwards to stand in front of the crowd.

The soldiers have woven together a crown out of thorny twigs and pushed it onto His head. They have thrown a purple robe around His shoulders, too. And they laugh and they smirk and they call out, 'Long live the King of the Jews!' And then they laugh again and they hit Him.

Once more Pilate cries, **'I CAN FIND NO REASON TO SENTENCE THIS MAN!'**

But this time, the chief priests and the guards from the Temple shout him down.

'Crucify Him! Crucify Him now!'

'You do it, then!' Pilate shouts back. 'I have no reason to!'

Still the crowd shouts. 'He claims to be the Son of God! Our Law says that means He must die!'

Now Pilate looks afraid.

He goes to Jesus. 'Where have You come from?' he demands. 'Don't You understand what power I have here? I have the power to set You free or to have You crucified!'

Jesus' voice is calm and quiet when He answers. 'The only reason you have any power over me at all,' He says, 'is because God gave you that power.'

The fear in Pilate's face grows deeper. Who is this Jesus? Why does He say the things He says?

Why is He prepared to *die like this*?

'Anyone who says they are a king,' screams the crowd at Pilate, 'is an enemy of our emperor. And if you set Jesus free, then you're an enemy of the emperor, too!'

Pilate stares out at them. They still shout but he can't make out the words anymore. It's just a noise that blasts through his head. A noise he cannot make sense of; a noise he just wants to stop.

Why can't this whole thing just stop ... and go away ...?

So finally Pilate does what they want.

## HE HANDS JESUS OVER TO THEM.

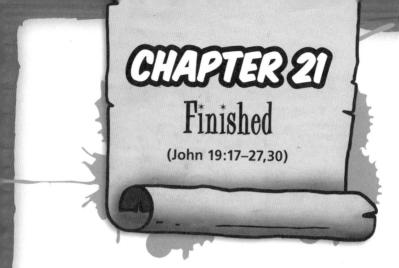

# CHAPTER 21

## Finished

### (John 19:17–27,30)

*I ran away, Jesus.*

There are grubby marks on Isaac's face. His cheeks are stained with tears. Grey-blue shadows circle under his eyes. He hasn't slept. He doesn't want to sleep. It's early morning, the third day since Jesus' death and every time he closes his eyes he sees the wooden cross; the hideous wooden cross that Jesus had to drag through the streets.

Before being nailed to it and left to die.

Isaac feels so empty. So empty and so lost.

Jesus is gone. And all he wants to do is talk to Him.

*After they arrested You in the garden, Jesus – I ran away.*

*Not because I don't care. Not because I don't love You – I do love You. I love You so much. I just didn't want to see what was going to happen. What Sarah said had to happen.*

*I didn't want to watch You die.*

*So I started to go back to my uncle's village. I told myself I didn't care if I never saw You again. I didn't care if I never saw the Topz Gang again either. All I cared about was not seeing You die.*

*I thought, I'll get back to my uncle's, I'll say goodbye to him, and then I'll head home to Capernaum. No point staying with my uncle anymore, I thought. I don't want to be a carpenter. Not now. Being a carpenter now would just remind me of You, and I didn't want to be reminded of You. I just wanted to forget You! Because if I could forget You, then it couldn't hurt. Knowing You were going to die – knowing You were going to give up Your life because of me, so that I could be with God forever – it couldn't hurt because You wouldn't be in my head. You wouldn't be in my heart. Maybe it could be as if I'd never seen You. Never listened to You. Never even heard of You.*

*As if You'd never been here at all.*

*But I didn't get very far, did I, Jesus? Because how can you run away from Someone who's with you and in you and all around you?*

*How could I run away from You, Jesus?*

*How could I run away from God?*

*That's who You are, isn't it? God sent You and He's a part of You and He's in You. You are God on the earth.*

*And however far I run, You will still be everywhere.*

*You've given me everything I have, and made the universe all around me. The sun, the moon, the stars, the skies, the oceans, the plains, the birds, the animals – they're all here because of You. Because You made them. You and Your Father God created everything I see. And everything I am.*

*So I stopped running.*

*And I came back.*

*I crept to the cross, Jesus.*

*I never thought wood could be used to make something so ugly. I saw the slash marks on Your skin where You'd been whipped; the gashes on Your head where the crown of thorns dug in.*

*I saw the nails they'd hammered into Your hands and into Your feet to hold You there. To pin You to Your cross.*

*I saw the notice the man Pilate wrote that he ordered to be put on the cross with You: 'Jesus of Nazareth, the King of the Jews'. Lots of people read it. And the chief priests told Pilate he should change it. They said, instead Pilate should write, 'This Man said I am the King of the Jews'.*

*But Pilate said no. He said what he'd written stayed written. It wasn't to be changed. Does he believe in You, Jesus? There must be a part of him that believes in You. But he still handed You over.*

*I watched the four soldiers who crucified You share Your clothes out between them. I watched them throw dice to see which one of them would get Your woven robe.*

*Your mother, Mary, was there, too. With her sister and another woman called Mary – Mary Magdalene. I've seen her before. Listening to You. She thought the world of You. I could always see it in her face. In her eyes.*

*And Your mother – I could hardly bear to look at her. I've never seen anyone with a heart that's so broken.*

*You called one of Your disciples over. You told him to look after her. You couldn't bear to see her so broken either. Could You …?*

*And then I stayed with You, Jesus.*
*I stayed with You until it was all over.*
*Until You said, 'It is finished!'*
*Until it really was.*
*Finished.*

*You told Your disciples not to be upset, Jesus. You told them not to be worried because one day they would see You again.*

*But when will that be, Jesus? When will any of us ever see You again? They've put Your body in a tomb and they've rolled a huge stone across the front.*

*You are hidden from us.*
*Torn from us.*
*You are gone.*

*And without You in it, it feels as though the world around me is* dead.

*Just as You are.*
*It's not supposed to be the end, Jesus.*
*But if it's not the end – where are You …?*

*'[Jesus] went out, carrying his cross, and came to "The Place of the Skull" … There they crucified him'*
*(John 19:17–18)*

# CHAPTER 22
## Breath of Life
### (John 20:1–16)

Someone's running.

Isaac hears the footsteps. He lifts his head where he sits. The ground underneath him is damp with morning dew, but he doesn't notice.

Who is it?

His eyes are tired. Sore from so much crying. He shoves his fists into them; rubs them hard. Blinks.

It's early to be running around. Way too early. *Who is it?*

Suddenly, there are more footfalls. Someone is behind him. Isaac's head whips round.

'Did you see them?' Paul stands there, breathing hard. 'Did you see them run past?'

'I don't know who it was,' says Isaac. 'What's going on?'

Paul is wide-eyed. He's breathless from running, too; breathless with uncertainty.

'Peter and another disciple,' he puffs. 'They're on their way to Jesus' tomb.'

Isaac frowns. Is he missing the point?

'So?' he grunts.

There are more running footsteps. Paul points and Isaac turns to see a woman. Her robe tucked up, she scurries along as fast as she can.

Isaac peers. 'Is that …?'

Paul nods. 'Mary Magdalene. And you'll never guess what, Isaac? I just heard her tell Peter and John that the stone's been moved!'

Isaac stares at him blankly. What's he talking about now? What stone?

Paul tuts and rolls his eyes. 'Oh, come on, Isaac, keep up! The stone in front of Jesus' tomb! It's been moved out of the way!'

Isaac takes a moment to let this news sink in.

Then instantly he's on his feet.

And the two boys run.

As they catch sight of the cave-like tomb, they slow. They stop. Mary's right. The stone isn't across the entrance anymore.

The disciple with Peter is already peering cautiously inside, but Peter just runs straight in. He looks all around, and comes out again. He looks at his friend; he looks at Mary, who has caught up with them.

He shakes his head. 'There's nothing there,' he says. 'Just the linen cloths Jesus' body was wrapped in. And the cloth around His head.'

'Someone's stolen Him!' hisses Isaac. 'Someone must have stolen Him!'

'But who?' mutters Paul. 'Why?'

Mary says something to the two disciples.

Isaac and Paul can't catch it. Then they watch as the two men, heads down, start to tramp away.

'Where are they going?' cries Isaac. 'Aren't they going to do something?'

'Ssh! Like what?' Paul shrugs his shoulders. 'What *can* they do?'

Mary doesn't follow. She stays outside the tomb. The boys can't see her face as it's turned away from them. But they can hear her sobbing.

They watch as Mary peers into the tomb. They move closer to try to get a look inside, too. A tree with a broad, rough-barked trunk stands close to the entrance. If they can just keep slightly to one side of it, perhaps they can see in without being spotted …

They suck in a sharp breath. Both together. They look at each other. They're not imagining it – they've both seen it.

Two figures dressed in white sit inside the tomb, exactly where Jesus' body would have lain. One where His head would have been and the other, His feet. As if they're marking the spot.

'Who's that?' Isaac whispers. 'There was no one there a minute ago. Peter would have said something. Who are they?'

Paul still stares. His mouth has dropped open.

'I think they're angels,' he murmurs. 'I don't even think – I *know* they're angels.'

One of the angels speaks to Mary. 'What's the matter? Why are you crying?'

Mary, choked with sobs, doesn't understand what she's seeing. She splutters, 'My Lord is gone …

I don't know where He is … They've taken His body away, and I don't know where He is!'

No one else speaks. For a few moments, there's no sound, just Mary quietly crying …

Neither Paul nor Isaac see the figure arrive. All of a sudden, someone just seems to be there – standing, back towards them.

As Mary turns slowly from the tomb, the figure is right in front of her.

He asks the same question as the angels: 'Why are you crying? Who are you looking for?'

Paul and Isaac freeze. They don't even breathe. They know the voice!

It's fantastic and mad and impossible, but *they know that voice* …

Mary's eyes brim with tears. She doesn't lift them to look at who is speaking to her. She is too full of grief. Too full of confusion.

'Is it you who's taken Him away, sir?' she sobs. 'If it is, then tell me where He is so that I can go and fetch Him.'

Isaac and Paul stare.

There's a pause. A tiny moment when still the very, very worst has happened and nothing seems possible anymore.

Until the figure speaks again: 'Mary!'

And then Mary lifts her face to His – and sees **JESUS!**

And early that morning, on the Sunday after Jesus' death, Isaac and Paul know that now everything is possible again because He is alive!

Jesus had died but He'd come back to life because *death couldn't hold Him!*

And the air around them moves gently as a light breeze lifts, and the dead earth heaves and starts to breathe again.

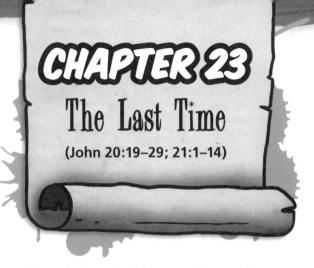

# CHAPTER 23
## The Last Time*
### (John 20:19–29; 21:1–14)

Topz walk on the beach with Isaac. The sea gleams turquoise-blue, reflecting the sky.

Isaac collects driftwood: small pieces that will fit into Sarah's bag. Sarah carries Saucy in her arms so that there's room inside. If Isaac's going to be a carpenter, he needs to practise. And if he's going to be able to practise, he'll need lots of wood.

The Gang don't talk much. They're happy just to be there. Together. The terrible thing has happened. But the terrible thing is over.

Jesus is alive again. Just as He'd promised He would be. There's nothing more they want.

All Jesus' disciples have seen Him now. He's promised them that the Holy Spirit – God's Spirit and their new Friend – will come to them soon.

He's got rid of any doubts that His coming back to life isn't real or is a lie. When His disciple, Thomas, demanded to see the scars of the nails in His hands – to touch the holes that they had made – Jesus let him. He had nothing to hide.

Jesus is the truth. And every word He has spoken is true, too.

Topz and Isaac – they understand why Jesus came. People had done so many wrong things. They'd ignored God for so long, it was as if they'd built a wall between themselves and Him. A wall of sin – wrong things and bad behaviour – so high and so wide that on their own they'd never be able to reach Him again.

So God sent Jesus to knock the wall down. He didn't want His people from the past – His people in the future – to have to live without Him because of the wrong they had done, and the wrong they would do.

Jesus would show people the way back to God.

Jesus would be *the way* back to God.

Instead of God punishing the people He had created, Jesus would take the punishment for all the sin in the world instead.

Jesus would suffer and die.

But then would come His glory!

God would bring Jesus back to life – to show that every word Jesus had spoken was true. He truly is God's Son. And to let everyone know that if they believe in Him, then they will live with God forever.

Gruff lifts his head. His nose twitches. In an instant he's pelting off up the beach.

John yells after him. 'Gruff! Gruff!'

Paul laughs. 'I'll get him,' and away he runs after him.

He catches up with the little dog when Gruff stops to sniff at some seaweed. He stoops to pick him up and as he straightens, he sees the disciples ahead of him on the beach.

They sit round a fire, eating and talking.

With Jesus.

Paul watches a moment. He smiles. Whenever Jesus is near, he feels safe. He feels loved.

He knows that the time will come, and soon, when Jesus will leave the earth. When Jesus will go back to be with His Father.

But he knows, too, that Jesus will never leave the world on its own. God's Holy Spirit will be there. And Jesus Himself, and His heavenly Father, will always be ready to listen. **TO LOVE.**

Gruff wriggles in his arms.

Paul takes a last look at Jesus. At the Man God sent. The Man who, on earth or in heaven, would always be his greatest adventure.

Then he turns and wanders back along the beach to his friends.

*'In his disciples' presence Jesus performed many other miracles ... But these have been written in order that you may believe that Jesus is the Messiah, the Son of God, and that through your faith in him you may have life.' (John 20:30–31)*

# Colourful daily Bible reading notes just for you

In each issue the Topz Gang teach you biblical truths through word games, puzzles, riddles, cartoons, competitions, simple prayers and daily Bible readings.

Available as an annual subscription or as single issues.

For current prices or to purchase go to **www.cwr.org.uk/store** call 01252 784700 or visit a Christian bookshop.